Northern & Western Counties

Edited by Annabel Cook

First published in Great Britain in 2005 by:
Young Writers
Remus House
Coltsfoot Drive
Peterborough
PE2 9JX
Telephone: 01733 890066
Website: www.youngwriters.co.uk

SB ISBN 1 84460 653 8

Foreword

Young Writers was established in 1991 and has been passionately devoted to the promotion of reading and writing in children and young adults ever since. The quest continues today. Young Writers remains as committed to engendering the fostering of burgeoning poetic and literary talent as ever.

This year's Young Writers competition has proven as vibrant and dynamic as ever and we are delighted to present a showcase of the best poetry from across the UK. Each poem has been carefully selected from a wealth of *Once Upon A Rhyme* entries before ultimately being published in this, our twelfth primary school poetry series.

Once again, we have been supremely impressed by the overall high quality of the entries we have received. The imagination, energy and creativity which has gone into each young writer's entry made choosing the best poems a challenging and often difficult but ultimately hugely rewarding task - the general high standard of the work submitted amply vindicating this opportunity to bring their poetry to a larger appreciative audience.

We sincerely hope you are pleased with our final selection and that you will enjoy *Once Upon A Rhyme Northern & Western Counties* for many years to come.

Contents

Lukes Lane Community Primary School Hebburn

Markland Hill CP School, Bolton

The Poems

My Cats

I have three favourite cats,
They're small, they're fun and cute,
They're always in the garden
And one of them's called Luke.

1 . . . 2 . . . 3
My favourite cats and me.

They're ginger, black and white,
They're happy all day long,
They always come to bed with me
And they're also very strong.

1 . . . 2 . . . 3
My favourite cats and me.

Jenna Cox (8)
Avishayes Community Primary School, Chard

The Magic Ring

I found a magic ring,
It's small and shines in the sun,
It's purple, blue and gold
And it likes to hum.

I rubbed the ring one day,
It turned into a genie,
I only had three wishes,
But then I had a freebie.

First I wished for lots of cash,
It didn't last me long,
Then I wished for big muscles
And I became very strong.

Hannah Jefferson (8)
Avishayes Community Primary School, Chard

Families

I love my family,
They're all mine
And when they go I cry,
But they're on time.

Families are fun,
You get lots of them.
Families are great,
But they drive you round the bend.

Emily Bartlett (7)
Avishayes Community Primary School, Chard

My Car

I love my favourite car,
It's very fast and fun,
The colours are dark and shiny,
They glitter in the sun.

It never makes me bored,
It skids across the floor,
It goes down my slide,
It goes out of the door.

Owen Pridden (7)
Avishayes Community Primary School, Chard

T-Rex Skeleton

I like my T-rex skeleton,
It is very tall.
It took me a long time to build it
And it stands against the wall.
When I go to bed
It wakes up at night,
It stands by my pillow
And it gives me a great fright.

James Dismore (7)
Avishayes Community Primary School, Chard

The Magic Necklace

I found a magic necklace,
It shines in the sun,
It's blue, yellow and red,
It looked like fun.

I put it on one day,
It whisked me away,
I ended up in Egypt,
Speaking Arabic quite a lot.

Anna Collins (8)
Avishayes Community Primary School, Chard

My Dog

I love my favourite dog,
She smiles through the day,
She's happy every year
And her birthday is in May.

My dog is called Molly,
She runs all day long.
My dog is very fast
And also very strong.

Luke Turner (8)
Avishayes Community Primary School, Chard

My Teddy

I love my favourite teddy,
I take him out the back
And we always play hide-and-seek
With my brother, Jack.
He's brown, black and white,
He's cuddly and soft,
He looks like silk
When I give him a wash.

Emily Newman (7)
Avishayes Community Primary School, Chard

My Teddy Bear

I love my favourite teddy bear,
It's fluffy, brown and soft,
Every night I sleep with her
And then I put her in the loft.

I took her out the loft,
We ran down the stairs,
We walked outside
And I combed Bear's hair.

Sadie Tillotson (8)
Avishayes Community Primary School, Chard

My Football

I love my favourite football
It keeps me very fit,
It is fun as long
As I don't get hit.
I practise every day,
Then the doorbell rings
And more come out to play.

Cory Slocombe (7)
Avishayes Community Primary School, Chard

My Sun Chair

I love my favourite sun chair,
I take it to the beach,
I will laze in it until
The sea touches my feet,
Then I go to sleep.
When I wake up,
I see I am floating on the sea.

Jodie Hannaford (7)
Avishayes Community Primary School, Chard

My Pets

I have two cats and guinea pigs,
The cats fight up our tree,
When I go to sleep in bed
They both snuggle up with me.

When I go and see the cats
They sometimes go all mad,
They start to jump around the room
And when I go they're sad.

The guinea pigs are hungry
And they always want to run,
They're nice, soft and fuzzy
But I just think they're fun.

Georgia Facey (8)
Avishayes Community Primary School, Chard

Football

My favourite sport is football,
I play it every day,
I play in my garden
When my friends come to stay.

We kick it to each other,
We kick it in the goal,
We all get excited
Because we scored a goal.

Lorna Brown (9) Michael Garland, Michael Symes (8) & Joshua Betts (7)
Avishayes Community Primary School, Chard

A Stormy Night

Wind, a fierce beast
Roaring like the wind;
Biting at your ears
With its big icicles
Running straight at you
Snarling in the darkness
Snapping the leaves off trees
With clashing teeth
Battering on the windows.

Rain, an angry beast
Scraping its claws against the;
Windowpane
Battering on your face
Like a person biting you
Slavering all over you
Like you have been
Soaked by the rain
What animal is it?

Matthew Bickerdike (9)
Burlington Primary School, Kirkby-in-Furness

A Beast Of A Storm!

The storm was a lashing lion
Pouncing on its prey,
The thunder was a tiger.
The wind as quick as wolves.

The storm set fire to the trees -
A dragon blowing fire on them.

Bradley Marshall (9)
Burlington Primary School, Kirkby-in-Furness

White Tup

Rough wind spread through the darkness.
The fierce white misty wool mixes with the absence like darkness.
Thunder made the beast's shadow fiercer.
The feet started to stamp on the muddy ground,
Eyes gleamed like a devil,
Horns struck by lightning, a fierce bounce of pain
Entered other people's minds
And then silent until the tide grew low.
People fled before the tup's sharp horns got them.
The head fell down, and rumbles shook the Earth.
Fork lightning struck the shining eyes,
What a terrifying night!
The strong wind blew the tup's head into the metal hurdles.
The fierce tup ran across the field for one purpose.
An electric pylon fell and tingled the wet legs.
Sheet lightning smashed the pylon end off.
Hounds of sheep running on the wet grass in a misty distance,
The rain hit the tup's wool, pulling it to the ground.
The tup could not see because of all the rain.

Daniel Armistead (10)
Burlington Primary School, Kirkby-in-Furness

The Wind

The wind roared like a lion attacking its prey.
Its mane stood up on end like a hedgerow.
The lightning struck and its eyes shone like car headlights!
Its teeth were like icicles hanging from a cave,
The blood dripped from its mouth,
Like raindrops from the sky.
Its tail swished like trees in the wind.
The lion moved stealthily like clouds rolling across the sky.
It pounced on the wildebeest,
Everything went quiet like the moon disappearing behind the clouds.

Andrew Benson (9)
Burlington Primary School, Kirkby-in-Furness

Fluffy Wind

Wind, a velvety kitten curled up on your lap
Disguised as a fluffy cushion until,
It turns round and pounces on you,
Scratching you with its needle-like teeth.
The sweet innocent pussy asleep in its bed
And when you turn around you find you're nearly dead!
It pounds like lightning as your bones crackle,
In fright, you scream, the cat just hisses
Getting ready to take its next bite.
Hiss, scratch, pounce, bite, goes the kitten in the night.
Kitty cat crawling round ruining everything in sight.
Blood splattering everywhere, death near close here.
The cat runs like shooting stars as the whole moon shines over us all,
Its fangs like bread knives, just a vampire flying in the midnight sky.

Sarah Wiejak (10)
Burlington Primary School, Kirkby-in-Furness

The Storm Of The Black Panther

Its tail whipped out of sight
And to its right.
A person stepped out of his home,
The panther shaped itself like a dome.
Its tail lashed the ground
Whilst its paws pawed the ground.
It crouched low to the ground ready to pounce,
It waited for the lightning to strike.
It pounced, blood fell,
A bone fell.
It leant over its dead prey,
The next day it had gone.

Ryan Tyson (10)
Burlington Primary School, Kirkby-in-Furness

Get Ready To Run!

His beady eyes disguised as lightning,
His cantering feet scrape like thunder.

His fur is like the freezing cold ice,
You can hardly see him from all the rain.

I hurl a stone at him, he's in pain!
The charging horse approaches me.

I get up on the horse, but it soon discards me,
Now I'm dead of course.

Buy maybe not, I might wake up
On the floor in the rain.
I'm in pain.

I see the horse, I get a dagger.
Blood was pouring from its eye,
The horse now gallops away
And from that day, it's never haunted me.

Lucy Harrison
Burlington Primary School, Kirkby-in-Furness

It's A Terrifying Night

Its teeth have pierced the night.
The rain trickles down like blood staining a gown.
Its purr is like a ripple of thunder far, far away
Edging closer to take its prey.
The wind is like a swish of a tail,
Don't go too close or your brain will go stale.

Emma Whitehead (10)
Burlington Primary School, Kirkby-in-Furness

The Black Shadow

The thunder growls
Like a dog.
People hide under
Their bed covers
And listen to
The wind's cry.
You peek out;
There's a black shadow
Of a dog, then you
Get out and look but
There's nothing there.
You turn around and
Then see the black
Dog waiting to
Pounce at you.
Run into your
Mum and dad's
Room but you're
Too late! They've
Already been
And gone.

Ellie Shepherd (9)
Burlington Primary School, Kirkby-in-Furness

Hunt For The Devil Bear

Bites like lightning,
Paws through the darkness,
Abyss like eyes contend with the darkness,
Tongue flickers out in never-ending malice,
Night quivers before it,
Red fangs rend and tear in flesh,
Blood spills brighter than the morning sun,
Eats its fill then moves on,
Kills and kills till its day is done,
Snores like thunder
Until it wakes,
Night-time prowling,
Kills its prey
Then returns to its bay,
Hunters attack,
Fires are lit,
Spears are sharpened,
Hunters shout,
Fangs snap,
People scream,
Animals roar,
Silence then until dawn!

Frederick Brock (10)
Burlington Primary School, Kirkby-in-Furness

Wolf Storm

Howling like a wolf
The wind screams around,
Biting anything exposed,
Scything leaves off trees,
Clawing off branches
With weapons of destruction,
Darkness spreads as fast as wolves striking,
Killing the life of day,
Senses quick as lightning strikes
With a growl as loud as thunder,
Pounces speedy as rain falls,
The rain falls like blood of a prey
Dripping to the floor
With a small splash,
Just the moonlight left to shine,
Hardly enough to see anything by,
Wolf scared by strength of light,
Just a little bit though
Eventually darkness backs away
Ready to bite another day.

Max Carruthers & Chris Littlechild (9)
Burlington Primary School, Kirkby-in-Furness

Leopard

A leopard
Running like a stampede,
His nose smoking
Like a red-hot boiler,
His claws sharp as kitchen knives,
His eyes glowing like St Elmo's fire.
His ears like big honkers,
His face is like a held hound's covered in blood,
Footsteps like thunder.
His spots like witches' warts,
His bony head like a rock
Sitting on its shoulder,
His tongue like a slimy serpent.
His tail lashes like a whip,
His legs are so fast you can only see the trail of dust behind him.

Jack Wilson (10)
Burlington Primary School, Kirkby-in-Furness

Horse Race

I see hooves,
I look up and see how fast it moves.
It is an amazing race,
The horse is going at a very fast pace,
I don't have time to see its face.
They are racing along the track,
The lady's giving the horse a smack.
Now the race is over and she's taking off her hat,
And giving the horse a well-deserved pat.

They are giving out the prizes
And some are strange surprises.

Emma Lumley (8)
Chewton Mendip CEVA School, Radstock

My Ambition

My ambition is to go round the world
With my best friend and our brothers
It's my dream as in my bed I curled
And I wouldn't do it with any others.

I imagine my knees were the mountains
My tummy's the desert below
My toy whale spurts out its fountains
My duvet's the blanket of snow.

My rugs are the very flat fish
Swimming in the carpet sea
My cushion boat's called The Starfish
And it's waiting in the quay.

And it was waiting right there
Eight years onwards or so
It was called The Flagstone
And she was comfy you know.

We flew right over Africa
Where the lions catch their prey
We sailed past the Galapagos Islands
Where the tortoise run and play.

We've met pirates and Indians,
We've discovered the Ellithong
And for all those who said we couldn't make it
We've gone and proved them wrong.

Hannah Jones (9)
Chewton Mendip CEVA School, Radstock

War

The war is here,
Why do people fight?
People suffering, dying even,
Why make people suffer?

I got evacuated in the second war,
The people I stayed with were horrid,
I suffered badly,
Why make people suffer?

Why can't we be joined?
The strongest army ever,
People are crying out names,
Why make people suffer?

Why do we kill people?
It's dreadful everyone dying,
Soon no one will be left,
Why make people suffer?

Please come to an end,
Why not be friends?
United together forever,
Why make people suffer?

Why do people fight?
Why can't we be friends?
Why do we kill people?
Why make people suffer?

Why can't we be joined together?
Standing together to the end,
No one's left, everyone's dead,
Why make people suffer?

Imogen White (9)
Chewton Mendip CEVA School, Radstock

Suffering

Blankets lying on the floor,
As I walk there are more and more,
Babies crying,
Adults dying,
What will happen?
What will happen?

As I looked around the street,
My heart seemed to lose a beat,
Children sleeping,
People weeping,
What will happen?
What will happen?

Ill people lying down alone,
I saw a man who had no home,
He was weeping,
Children sleeping,
What will happen?
What will happen?

People lying down beside doors,
I thought they looked really poor,
A lady sleeping,
In her sleep she was weeping,
What will happen?
What will happen?

Walking down the streets of Bath,
I couldn't even force a laugh,
Babies screaming,
Nothing gleaming,
What will happen?
What will happen?

Mark Fitzsimmons (9)
Chewton Mendip CEVA School, Radstock

Will You Ever Learn?

As I looked out of the window
The sight I saw came as no shock
The smell of smoke and charred buildings
Damaged boats waiting at the dock

I could see that in the next village
It was lit up with streaks of flame
All that it took was that one deathly bomb
And the whole village was destroyed again

The First World War was bad enough
But the second brought terror and pain
Tears were shed from every family
What on earth is there to gain?

Yells of pain filled the air
A big explosion was heard nearby
This is how I met my death
It was pointless, why oh why?

As I watch you all now from Heaven
I wonder if you'll ever learn
You're still fighting and killing each other
And leaving your houses to burn

It makes me weep to remember
That day the war began
Will you not be happy
Until you have destroyed every man?

That day the war began . . .

Virginia Gay (9)
Chewton Mendip CEVA School, Radstock

The Green Seagull

One day I saw a flock of seagulls
The most beautiful sight I'd seen,
I noticed that one looked quite different
Not white, but emerald green.

The seagulls flew closer towards me
High over the bay,
The green bird suddenly swooped down
He was coming my way.

His wings sparkled in the sunlight
His eyes as black as night,
He had something golden in his beak,
It was such a beautiful sight.

But then I saw in his beak
Was a golden, struggling fish,
The fish squirmed in the seagull's beak
With his tail going lash, crash, bash.

The seagull came down to land beside me,
What was it going to do?
I was amazed that I could see something so magical,
Colourful too.

Huw Thomas (9)
Chewton Mendip CEVA School, Radstock

Gymnastics - Haiku

I did somersaults
I'm good on the trampoline
I can do the splits.

Ben Morgan (9)
Chewton Mendip CEVA School, Radstock

I'm Curious

There are mysteries never to be solved
A key to an answer . . .

There're so many things I want to know
And so much to find out.
Questions and mysteries are all around
They can't all have answers, no doubt.

How many stars are there in the sky?
Is there such a place as Hell?
Does God know the future? Do scientists lie?
If you know please tell!

Millions of questions, loads and loads.
How does Heaven look?
Are there answers? Who really knows?
Could we find out in a book?

How many fish in the sea?
What is good?
Who made me?
I could think of loads of questions, I know I could.

I'm curious!

Nicola Terrell (9)
Chewton Mendip CEVA School, Radstock

Poland - Haiku

It is very cold,
It has polar bears that swim,
They will eat people.

Daniel Blackman (9)
Chewton Mendip CEVA School, Radstock

The War

War is here, now the word is clear,
The colours of the flames,
The screaming and the pain,
The war is here once again.
It was a joke at first but now it is real,
We all get down, crouch or kneel,
Pray to the Lord, let it be OK,
For the war will come either way.
The hills stand still, mist wrapped around,
When from behind comes a terrible sound.
Planes come out, I start to shout,
My school was in flame,
My mum was insane.
The war was bad,
Everyone was sad.
There was blood on the floor,
What is the reason for all this war?

Alice Walker (9)
Chewton Mendip CEVA School, Radstock

Space

As I look from my room,
I can see the shining moon.
Then I think of a twinkling star,
I wonder how big they all are?
I wonder how many people have been in space?
I wonder if they're seen in every single place?
I wonder if you can see your house?
I wonder if you can see a mouse?
It must be high up in the sky,
I wonder if you can see the birds fly by.

Nia English-Webb (9)
Chewton Mendip CEVA School, Radstock

The Deer

It stood right in front of me tall and fair,
This deer had silky golden hair.
I found his back really smooth,
And then it made a dashing move.

Leaping, prancing, urging me on,
I just had to climb upon.
We went racing through the woods at top gear,
I thought I smelled a hunter near . . .

Bang! Bang! Bang! went the hunter's gun,
It made my deer really run.
I heard the noise of his car,
I could tell he wasn't very far.

Suddenly my deer fell in a heap,
And I started to weep.
The old man comforted me,
And I went back to his house for tea.

Ben Watts (9)
Chewton Mendip CEVA School, Radstock

My Ride On My Horse

I was galloping through the trees,
When I saw a dog with fleas.
I looked at my horse's mane,
I stopped, he was lame.
Then I led him home,
I got another horse on loan.
I sat on my new horse,
I galloped round the course.
He bucked me off,
I started to cough.
I got back on,
I started to sing a song.

Holly Clothier (8)
Chewton Mendip CEVA School, Radstock

Tornado

Where have all the birds gone?
There's nothing in the sky
But as I look more closely
The clouds are flying by.

The wind is getting stronger,
It's howling round the house,
I can hear the windows rattling,
I'm as frightened as a mouse.

I think it's getting quieter,
I'll take a sneaky look,
There's leaves and branches everywhere
No wonder the house shook.

The clouds are slowly parting,
There's blue sky up above.
I think I hear the birds now
I even see a dove.

Grant McConnell (9)
Chewton Mendip CEVA School, Radstock

Rugby - Haiku

Pass the rugby ball,
My stud came out, I lost it,
I scored a drop-kick.

Keiran Perrin (9)
Chewton Mendip CEVA School, Radstock

Big Old Space

Space, space great big space,
It looks just like a gigantic face.
Bigger than Earth, bigger than the moon,
I want to visit, but not that soon.

Mars, Mars, giant Mars,
A planet just beyond the stars.
Pluto, Pluto, the very smallest,
But if you stretch it, it would be the tallest.

No humans except astronauts,
I have been one in my thoughts.
I will be one when I'm an adult,
My rocket won't have a single fault.

I want to fly to the moon
The rocket will blast off at 12 noon.
I will fly past the stars
I will fly to Venus, I will fly to Mars.

Benjamin Jones (8)
Chewton Mendip CEVA School, Radstock

Gods - Haiku

The gods are mighty,
They live in the cave of rock.
We pray for the gods.

Zak Sanger-Reynolds (9)
Chewton Mendip CEVA School, Radstock

The War

As I sat alone I heard the sound of gun men pelting,
And tank tracks squelching,
Babies screaming, nothing gleaming,
Slim and thin people with their blankets at our door,
There's nothing to laugh about, this is the war.

There are army men out there with their guns,
They really had to run to get the job done.
You could say everyone was poor,
There's nothing to laugh about, this is the war.

When will this stop?
I think in my mind I heard Hitler's plot.
I walked down the drive and looked
On the ground there was lots of mud
But also lots and lots of blood.
I've got to the last core,
There's nothing to laugh about, this is the war.

Jack Schneider (9)
Chewton Mendip CEVA School, Radstock

Sports

I run, I kick, I score
That goal number four.
The football team all shouted and cheered
Celebration is all I hear.

I run, I scrum, I slide
Over the line I dive.
Rugby is my game,
Joseph is my name.

I run, I bounce, I jump
And land with a thump
I score a goal - 25 points to Wales
They won the match, teamwork never fails.

Joseph Morgan (9)
Chewton Mendip CEVA School, Radstock

Winter

I looked out the window,
The lawn was covered in snow,
It was as though somebody had covered it in a
Big white blanket and crows in a row,
The snow makes me go blue, it is so cold,
The sun is shining and shimmering like gold,
But soon the sun will go down and the sky will be grey,
And then it will be the end of another winter's day,
Animals are hibernating in their cosy nests,
Out of all the seasons winter is the best,
Playing on our wooden sledges,
Crashing into spiky hedges,
Crunching snow under people's feet,
And playing with the children that we meet,
Sitting by the fire the flames burning red,
I cuddle up tight and go to bed.

Lucy Berry (9)
Chewton Mendip CEVA School, Radstock

The Owl

The owl flutters around at night,
Giving mice one good fright!
Flying back through all the sticks,
Going back to feed her chicks.
The day has come to learn to fly,
High, high into the sky.
'Well done, well done, you've passed the test,
Now let's fly back to the nest.
I hope you're hungry, ready for tea,
Now stay here and wait for me.'
She gave a little cry and then
Flew into the night sky.

Menna Waites (10)
Chiseldon Primary School, Swindon

Petal Rain

The rain lands on me softly
with its gentle touch of love.

The grass shines bright and green
like when the winds blow
and push the petals off.

Stephanie Wilkins (10)
Chiseldon Primary School, Swindon

Night

Night is a gentle fairy,
She makes me feel peaceful and calm.
Her face looks kind
Her eyes are twinkly
Her mouth is silent.
Her hair sparkles
Her clothes are made of silk
She moves as soft as a kitten.
When she speaks it sounds like music,
She lives in a garden with flower beds and kittens
Night cuddles me.

Chantelle Crossley (10)
Edenfield CE School, Bury

Night

As he creeps over the world, leaving it in darkness,
He sweeps the streets, filling all the houses with sleep.
As he covers the world in darkness,
When his work was complete
The light fought back and ruined
All his hard work.

Paul Pemberton (10)
Edenfield CE School, Bury

Night

Night clothes the silent streets.
A haggered witch with a croaky voice,
Swirls around the misty corners.
Drifting through the icy roads.
She smothers the house with her ragged cloak.
Night dives down a steep road casting spells on little children.
Then suddenly the wolves howled calling to each other in the
Gloomy woods.
Dancing trees swayed while the wind blew dangerously.
Night is drawing nearer to the sun and the world is changing.
When the light fights the dark as morning comes, the witch
Hides in her cosy home.
Sunrise came and the tropical flowers shone like a rainbow.
The rivers flowed like the wind and the light of the sun sparkled upon it.

Samantha Clarke (10)
Edenfield CE School, Bury

Night

The creepy ghost trembles the street,
Scaring people that he meets.
Torn clothes that he wears
Ripped by wind and slashed by storms.
He lives on hills and seaside rocks,
Battered by sea and crushed to sand.
He stumbles to the street
The ghost smacks the house
When evening is past
Leaving darkness where he walks
Hours later when the sunrise blooms,
He has gone
For day and gone until night.

Samuel Bentley (11)
Edenfield CE School, Bury

Night

As the night rose over the hill
As the call of the wolves howled,
the silent meadow lights up with the creeping moonlight,
stared over the icy waterfall with the grey mist.
The green grass gleamed in the moonlight,
the trees swayed in the midnight sky.
Slowly but surely the sweet little girl crept up
and jumped off a nearby tree.
Her face was as white and cold as snow.
Her dress was as bright as the burning sun
Her hair flows long and brown.

One by one the lights in the town are switched off,
she creeps up on windows to make sure everyone's asleep.

She storms over fences and trees and covers everything in sight
with stars and darkness.

But suddenly, she blends into the night sky as the sun rises
for the new day.
Never to return until moonlight.

Amy Hollis (10)
Edenfield CE School, Bury

Night

Night is an old man
He makes me feel old and grumpy
His face looks wrinkly like a worm
His eyes are twinkling
His mouth is toothless
His hair, curly, short and grey
His clothes are made of old sheepskins
When he moves he shuffles silently
When he speaks he croaks like a frog
He lives in an old hut with dogs and mice.
Night scares me.

Philip White (10)
Edenfield CE School, Bury

Night

Night is a dark witch with a black cat
Creeping up on you.
Suddenly frightening you into a deep, dark sleep.
Wearing a black cloak that covers one half of the midnight world.
Whistling wildly to its strong friend the wind.
It is angry, slithers somewhere pitch-black.
Sneaks up on you and makes it invisible.
Its cloak like the teacher's blackboard.
It has star teeth and a moon face that shines brightly.
Blinds are blocking out the light around the huge world.
The wicked witch creeps in your bedroom
Wakes your toys then play together
Sometimes awakening you by mistake.
The light fades not yet nine o'clock
Beware the wicked witch of the pitch-black night
Coming towards you . . .
Watch out!

Bethany Fulcher (10)
Edenfield CE School, Bury

Night

Night is a dark king creeping up on the happy sun,
Enveloping it with his long black cloak.
Following fearless little children,
Eating up all the fluffy clouds.

The night is coming,
Now the dark king comes out.
Spreading darkness all over the streets
In the towns and in the football grounds.

The dark king hides,
In his home in a haunted, silent castle.
The sun is rising once again.

Mark Rooth (10)
Edenfield CE School, Bury

Night

Night becomes a mysterious girl,
Her eyes are as stars,
She moves silently like a mouse.
Night has a face like a silver fog crawling over the sky,
She makes you feel relaxed, calm and warm.

Into the darkness,
She evolves into an evil witch
And has a cape of silver stars that covers us.
Night makes chirping chicks drift into a new world of sleep.

As dawn approaches,
The witch turns into the mysterious girl she used to be.
But now she is no longer the night, she is a summer goddess.

Grace Davis (10)
Edenfield CE School, Bury

Night

Night is a fierce magician who terrifies me.
His hair a battered mop
Flashing eyes as red as blood
His face is as terrifying as a horror movie.
His teeth are small and razor-sharp.
His fingers are like bold twigs
Wearing clothes of deer's skin
When he moves his black cloak strides along the floor.
When he speaks the ground shakes under him
He lives in a dark and gloomy tower
With a black cat and an ugly toad.
Night scares me.

Maverick Brierley (10)
Edenfield CE School, Bury

Night

Slowly, silently, darkness looms over you.
It creeps quietly, swinging its jet-black cloak over everything.
Like a duvet, clothing everything in total darkness.
It seeks senselessly, putting everything in its path to sleep.
It sneaks up like a fox on the sun and takes over.
Night arrives.

Creeping up on the street, clothing you in a mantle of silvery stars.
Staring down, he chills you in your sleep.
Leaves you hoping he will go away.
The silver moonlight shoots in to make it light.
As morning dawns the lord shrinks back into his cave
awaiting another day.

James Boott (11)
Edenfield CE School, Bury

Night

He throws his cloak of coldness over the earth,
The lord of night-time muffles all action in a cloud of darkness.
His sworn enemy is the daylight,
Moonlight floods into the sky of the lord.
Night's friends are wind and rain,
They help to cause destruction and danger.
In the late hours Night explores the snowy mountain peaks,
He tosses the glittering stars into the dark midnight sky.
When morning comes Night hides in the rocky caves,
But he soon returns.
Even though Night doesn't like light,
He uses the moon to see chaos he has caused.

Joseph Wallwork (10)
Edenfield CE School, Bury

Night

The creepy darkness shrouds the school,
advancing on to its next victim, the silent street.
Before drifting back to its haunted house,
where only the sun can attack.
The ghost wore a plain white cloak,
spreading darkness across the world.
His eyes are as red as blood.
He is as dangerous as a slithery snake.
He is like a leopard leaping for his prey.
Darkness grows as time passes.
Now the people are deeply dreaming.
As the sun peeps through,
the dark clouds part as day dawns.
The phantom evaporates . . .

Andrew Fernando (10)
Edenfield CE School, Bury

Night

She is the relaxing midnight sky,
She covers us with a dishcloth of darkness.
She silently checks us when we are sleeping.
A gentle nanny protecting her children.

She sparkles all through the night,
Her eyes glow in the icy blackness.
Glowing, she makes sure that every child can see their way.

As a new day dawns she blends into the summer breeze,
Until the next night, when she is needed again.

Katy Common (10)
Edenfield CE School, Bury

Night

Suddenly the night witch wrapped the forest in a big, soft blanket.
The night's black and silver cape covered the haunted hills
of Cornwall.
The night's eyes gleamed in the shadowy moonlight.
Her feet crept past the bear's cave.
The night caught a ladybird and swallowed it whole.
Then the owl flew past a silver, gleaming waterfall,
As the mice scattered through the flower beds.
The wolves howled at the blue moon.
The wind whipped the fir trees with anger,
but the trees lost the battle to the wind.

Rebecca Barrow (10)
Edenfield CE School, Bury

Night

The dark witch creeps on the misty roads,
She flies through the dark, dank sky.
Night is like a wicked witch
Whose long cloak drifts through the silent street.
When morning comes the night dies,
The witch flies through the morning sky.
The golden sunshine gleams in the misty sky.
She speaks with a croaky voice,
When she flies her mouth is silent.
Her faces looks horrible and wrinkly.

Rebecca Farnworth (10)
Edenfield CE School, Bury

Night

The dark lord creeps through the tired town,
forcing his presence through the open windows.
He is like a cloak protecting all that it touches.
Moonlight gleaming through the alleyways
like a lantern held by a phantom ghost.
Clothes torn by the whistling wind.
Minutes later the sunrise fights back,
sweeping the stars with a new broom.

Isaac Campbell (10)
Edenfield CE School, Bury

Mr Hall!

Mr Hall was the best in the school,
He wasn't a teacher,
But he really did rule.

He was the caretaker,
And he was ace,
He would clean everywhere,
Yep, every single place.

Now he isn't with us,
He is at a different school,
It's down the road
Just being built,
And we will miss him so.

We had to say goodbye to him,
We had a special mass,
We said, 'Bye-bye.'
And gave him a gift
And that is when he went.

Hannah Roocroft (10)
Holy Family RC Primary School, Wigan

Summer Is Hot!

Summer is hot!
I am going to France,
I'll go in a bar but I will not dance.

I won't eat frogs' legs
And definitely not snails,
I'll stay in the caravan all day
Playing heads or tails.

Not! I'll enjoy myself all week
And at the end I will not peek
Out the place
Out the place and when I do
I'll feel so bleak.

Helena Culshaw (10)
Holy Family RC Primary School, Wigan

My Dog Sam

My dog Sam
Is a very jolly man
He jumps up and down
And runs around and around.
He barks all night and he barks all day
Until we let him out to play!
He's black and tan
With big white paws
When he jumps up
Ouch! Watch those claws.
I love my Sam!
I'm his number one fan!

Hannah Regan (8)
Holy Family RC Primary School, Wigan

The Flood

The sparkling sun,
The sparkling sun,
How I loathe her,
The sparkling sun!

Shining so brightly,
Up in the sky,
Striding along,
For the people passing by.
But I am joyful,
For ruining her praise,
By flooding the town,
With my evil ways!

The sparkling sun,
The sparkling sun,
How I loathe her,
The sparkling sun!

The people adore her,
It's unbearable to me,
With her smiling face,
She's better than us three.
The poor wind,
All alone,
Nobody likes him,
That they've all shown.

The sparkling sun,
The sparkling sun,
How I loathe her,
The sparkling sun!

We'll get her back,
For what she's done,
To me and the wind,
The match we've won.
The wind will take over,
But right now he's too low,
To be cool enough for king,
But he might be in 3004!

The sparkling sun,
The sparkling sun,
How I loathe her,
The sparkling sun!

Rebecca Edwards (11)
Holy Family RC Primary School, Wigan

Chatterbox!

I'm a chatterbox
I talk all day.
I talk all night
And in my sleep I give people frights.

I'm a chatterbox
I never shut up
I talk for hours
Even when I am watching TV.

I'm a chatterbox
I get told off in class
I don't give a toss
When I do my maths.

I'm a chatter box
I run up the bill
My mum and dad shout at me
I don't care because I don't pay the bill.

Abbey Joyce & Chloe Warburton (10)
Holy Family RC Primary School, Wigan

I'm A Bully

I'm a bully don't mess wi' me
If you do I'll eat you for ma' tea
(Well, not really)

I'm a bully don't mess wi' me
If you do you'll have to pay a fee
(Well, only 5p)

I'm a bully don't mess wi' me
If you do I'll break your knee
(Well, kick it)

I'm a bully and I'm well 'ard
Mess wi' me and . . . and
and . . . erm . . .
(Oh well, nowt)

Anna McKay & Hannah Roocroft (11)
Holy Family RC Primary School, Wigan

My Day

Early in the morning on a warm, clear day,
Getting ready for school and on my way,
As I work hard and try my best,
At home time I'm ready for a well-earned rest.
Looking through my window
I see the beautiful flowers
Listening to music and dancing for hours,
Playing with Robyn and seeing Ellie smile,
Walking in the autumn woods, mile after mile,
Late at night when the stars shine bright,
God is there to say goodnight.

Anna McKay (11)
Holy Family RC Primary School, Wigan

Super-Woman

I'm Super-Woman
I save everyone
Lots of people love me
(well, some of them)

I'm Super-Woman
I can fly from place to place
My red and blue robes gliding in the air
(well, they're my jeans and my rugby shirt really)

I'm Super-Woman
I could save the whole world
I'd put out all the fires
(if the fire brigade hadn't arrived)

Beth O'Grady (10)
Holy Family RC Primary School, Wigan

The Wind

Huge angry and ferocious
Pushing everything in its way
Desperate to destroy.

The wind is a bully.

A horrible force of nature
A force to be reckoned with
It thrusts everything in its way.

The wind is a bully.

Faster than the speed of sound
The wind hates everyone.

The wind is a bully.

Joe Croston (10) & Robert Culshaw (11)
Holy Family RC Primary School, Wigan

Tornado

Power,
Wailing,
Twisting,
Tornado blows against the houses of New York
Trying to destroy
Ready to plot revenge.

Huge,
Strong,
Vicious,
Tornado blows against the houses of America
Prepared to destroy
Ready for revenge.

Aisling McMullen (11)
Holy Family RC Primary School, Wigan

The Clouds

T he clouds up there so very high
H anging down from the sky
E very single day I see

C louds that appear before me
L ovely clouds look like cotton wool balls
O h can you hear those angel calls
U nicorns leap over those clouds
D o you hear? Listen, listen to the sound
S o very soft while someone's around.

Katharine Lamb (10)
Holy Family RC Primary School, Wigan

My Wonderful Gran

My gran has perfumed slippers.
She walks around spraying perfume all over the house.
When she's bored she sorts all her make-up
and tries them all on herself.
Oh how pretty my gran looks!

When my gran goes out everyone bows and says,
'Oh you look lovely today.'
My gran wears wonderful clothes and shoes that glitter in the sunlight.
My gran looks lovely today!

My gran is just like the queen, she speaks so highly.
She is neat like the queen, she dresses perfectly like the queen.
I love my gran so much.

My gran is so perfect I love her so much.
She loves everyone around her like they love her.

Amiee Hanna (9)
Holy Family RC Primary School, Wigan

Dolphin!

There is a dolphin
Jumping gracefully
Diving under the sun
Smiling happily.
The silky-smooth grey-blue
Skin shining once again
I waved to it
It waved to me
Then it went back down
To the bottom of the sea.

Chloe Warburton (10)
Holy Family RC Primary School, Wigan

Revenge!

Fast flowing river
Rising steady to seek revenge
And destroy everything
That gets in its way.

Powerful, ferocious
The rushing river thrashes its banks
Trying to smash its prison
And barge down the walls.

Angry, monstrous, energetic
The river takes everything with it
But now the river has calmed down
It will never seek revenge again.

Nathan Renouf (11)
Holy Family RC Primary School, Wigan

Dexter The Dog!

Dexter is brown and white
He likes to play, but will never bite.
His fur is soft and fluffy too
He likes to play with his toy shoe.
On the field he runs about
To get him back you have to shout.
When he's poorly we take him to the vet
Because *Dexter* is my pet!

Abbey Joyce (10)
Holy Family RC Primary School, Wigan

I Hate School Dinners

Rubber chips that make people do the flips,
Spider pie that makes you say bye-bye.
Stale jelly that tastes like bellies,
Teachers with sticks that are used for whips,
Mouldy biscuits, cold tea,
Custard that looks like mustard,
Rolled up rolls with bowling balls,
Oh why, oh why do we have to eat school dinners?

Melissa Rollins (10)
Holy Family RC Primary School, Wigan

Rabbit

There it stares
For hours on end.
Then hopping gracefully
In its own space.
Its ears flapping
This way and that
With its fur so soft
Nudging me till the break of day.

Ruby Melling (10)
Holy Family RC Primary School, Wigan

I Want That!

I want that book, I want to cook,
I want that toy, not that boy,
I want that power, I want that flower
I want that tree as big as me.
I want everything!

Robyn Yates (8)
Holy Family RC Primary School, Wigan

Smells

In the morning I wake up to smell wonderful smells.
I smell a rose, I smell petals, I smell grass, it reminds me of spring.
I hate the smell of petrol, I hate the smell of smoke,
But most of all I hate the smell of my dad's cigars.
I like the smell of pop, I like the smell of fizz,
But most of all I like the smell of wine when I dine.
I hate the smell of dogs, I hate the smell of mice,
But most of all I hate the smell of my cousin's hamster.

Francesca Rigby (9)
Holy Family RC Primary School, Wigan

Early Morn

The sleeping flowers begin to uncurl
Their golden petals to the early sunrise,
Clouds begin to gradually move
Like ghostly galleons across the crystal-blue sky,
God washes away pale, pastel pink skies into blotches of blue,
Many poor, unwealthy families open their sleepy eyes
To the harsh, gruelling world around them,
Frosty, glittering cobwebs hang like soft, swaying hammocks
In the delicate wind
A stuttering lorry grunts as it has to embark on another exhausting
Journey to where its driver desires to go
As the pastel yellow moon fades away
The colours of the sun sprinkle a radiant,
Waking glow on all who seek it.

Katie Gledhill (10)
Hutton Rudby Primary School, Yarm

The Awakening Of The Morn

The cars eyes gently shut to a silent standstill,
The people stir in their beds
As the silhouetting sun rises over the weary hills,
The street lamps, one by one, go off like stars on a frosty morn,
From the branches of an oak tree
The crispy leaves descend to the dewy grass below,
The dustbin lorry takes its journey further on as it spurts into life,
The blackbird sings its sweet melody as daybreak begins,
The trees sway gently in the wind like a clock's second hand,
Tick-tick-ticking.
Now daybreak has begun yet again.

Niall Innes (11)
Hutton Rudby Primary School, Yarm

Ode To Autumn

Hast thou seen leaves weeping to the ground?
Crunch, crunch, crunch, I hear a sound,
Yonder stubble swinging side to side,
Painted skies, blue and white, dazzling in thine sunlight.
The frost setting on the grass.

Hast thou seen the clouds set upon the sky,
Like a baby lays upon their cot?
Hedgehogs hibernate in the breeze
Conkers falling from the trees,
All these things doth come in autumn time,
Winter's icy fingers come creeping across the grass.

Jessica Roberts (10)
Hutton Rudby Primary School, Yarm

Mutant Goldfish

I've got a pet mutant goldfish
He smells like a piece of old radish.

It's a slimy, orange and lime
It's died a whopping one time
Once I saw him have a dance
He pretended his hand was a lance
He has got his own collar
He bought it for a dollar
Once I saw him using a thread and sew
The next day I saw a floating toe
Once he tried to play the clarinet
But it didn't work because it was soaking wet.

I've got a mutant goldfish
He smells like a piece of old radish.

Chris Howell (10)
Hutton Rudby Primary School, Yarm

Grandma

Her twinkling eyes tell her future dreams,
Her toothless mouth causes a lopsided grin,
Consistently telling me how tall I'm getting.

Her wrinkles tell you her good times from the past,
Her fingers slipping sideways with arthritis,
Consistently asking me how old I am
But that's just Grandma!

Emma Rettig (10)
Hutton Rudby Primary School, Yarm

The Dawning Light

The sun rose to give light to the long, dreary night,
Stars flicker and fade like a candle being blown out,
The moon finally giving way to let the bright light in,
The car stuttering and coughing in the graceful glow of the
morning sun,
The blood-red clouds drifting away to let a shaft of shining sunlight in,
The birds waking up to give their early morning call,
Ready for the day to begin,
The sun starting to shine happily for the new day,
The ageing acorn tree opened passage
For the golden, bright beam of light,
The sun shone with pride on the village below,
The long night has finally been released from the world.

Mark Libby (10)
Hutton Rudby Primary School, Yarm

If I Were The Queen

If I were the Queen,
I'd have never-ending jewels,
A thousand servants
And a McDonald's next door.

If I were the Queen,
I'd have a fairground with the scariest rides,
The very looniest circus
And one of those electric beds that go up and down.

If I were the Queen I'd have all of these!

Abigail Brown (10)
Hutton Rudby Primary School, Yarm

The Border Refugee

He stood there in the corner,
Matchboxes in his hands.
Selling them's his game,
He's forgotten his name.

His clothes are rags,
His leg is broken,
He hobbles on.
I don't know where he lives -
Imagine it's not much.

His legs are thin,
His belly fat.
The effect of bloatage.

He has no family,
He has no rights,
No identity,
He's another refugee.

James Thorniley-Walker (10)
Hutton Rudby Primary School, Yarm

Summer

Spring dies into the mist, the world,
Summer's born, begins to rise and stare down onto the world,
Painted sun, glowing sky,
Spring has gone, come to die,
Next is autumn, cold with frost,
Summer's gone, now it is lost.

Alice Hughes (10)
Hutton Rudby Primary School, Yarm

Daybreak

The moon, like a pale washed-out figure glides across the sky,
drifting dreamily through the clouds.
The sparkling lights of a city, gradually fade one by one
as the world becomes silent.
Many baby animals cautiously creep out of hides
to see the world for the first time.
An owl, quietly watches over the world
like a reliable guardian to God's children.
Lazily people slumber in their soft, cosy beds,
not wanting to get up and face the new dawn.
Gradually the sun makes its appearance glowing softly
over a crystal clear lake magnifying every unique raindrop.
A spider delicately tiptoes across its wavering cobweb
not wanting to break a single lacy thread.
Daybreak has finally come!

Laura Simpson (10)
Hutton Rudby Primary School, Yarm

My Class

Hugh and George are like two silly twins,
they are always messing around
And then there's Mr Robinson he doesn't like to shout,
Jessica can never stop singing,
Grace gallops like a horse in a fuss,
Mrs Hoyle is always there to help you,
Alice is the tallest, definitely not the smallest,
Then there's Helena and she loves to dance about,
Also Paige who loves to play football,
My class is the best, I don't want to leave them!

Georgina Nicholson (10)
Hutton Rudby Primary School, Yarm

The Dentist

Tomorrow I'm off to the dentist
The teeth destroying apprentice.
What a smelly place it is
It will make your mouth froth and fizz.

Mum says it will help
But I know I will yelp.
Everyone's laughing at me at school
Because it's totally uncool.

'Prepare to die,' they all say
But wait until they have to pay
Their teeth will be big and green
And smell of gasoline!

Once they visit the dentist
The teeth destroying apprentice.

Tom Hargreaves (11)
Hutton Rudby Primary School, Yarm

The Monster

The monster is a bushy, red beast,
The last of its kind,
It has two long, sharp teeth sticking out of its mouth
Its claws are jagged
It likes to wear a pair of old, ripped shorts
And it has small devil-like horns growing out of its head
If you ever see this monster, just run away screaming
Or else it'll try and get you!

Lewis Deans (10)
Hutton Rudby Primary School, Yarm

Doom

While you're tucked up in bed,
When the clock strikes midnight,
Walking through the streets,
Comes Doom the wanderer,
He wears a black coat and hood
And a grey cloak,
Which hangs down to brown leather boots,
He grips a Mack II in his left hand,
His only means of protection,
A scar runs down his neck
As he passes a birdhouse
He grabs a handful of seeds,
Opens his mouth to eat it, showing jagged teeth,
Slowly he smiles as he sees a door arch,
This will be his bed.

Rory Duncan (10)
Hutton Rudby Primary School, Yarm

Daybreak

God gets his paint palette out
and paints the fresh colours into the morn,
The old, rusty morning lorry
drags itself across the empty road,
The lazy city wakes up from a long night
and people groan out of bed.

The trees look up to the sun and smile
The dramatic clouds unveil the blue, velvet sky,
The sun filters through the trees to start the day.
The sun is here, it is morn.

Jo Bainbridge (10)
Hutton Rudby Primary School, Yarm

The Grumpet

The grumpet is a monstrous beast
He measures three feet at least
His legs are short and stubby
And his clothes are really grubby.

His fangs are long and sharp
And he feeds on plaice and carp
His rear end stinks
And in the night he slinks around and around his rock.

He watches travellers stroll by
He dreams and dreams of human pie
He carries a brutal, pointy club
His pet is a vicious wolf cub.

One day hunters came through town
Saw him running, shot him down
The wood was filled with his bloodshed
For now the grumpet was full of lead.

William Readman (11)
Hutton Rudby Primary School, Yarm

The Gift Of Peace

A plague of sunshine crusaders around the majestic autumn's edge
The tribes of young fox cubs gracefully wait for their mother
For a successful catch.
A hungry baby fills the chilled air with a soft cry
like an oozing fan on a hot day.
It is night but in this magical world it is never dark
The mountain peaks for the end of autumn has come.

Angus Ralph Wilsdon (11)
Hutton Rudby Primary School, Yarm

The Break Of Day

The moon gleamed over the sleepy town
Like a street lamp flickering in an empty street.
The ancient oak tree quivered in the frosty darkness
As the godly steeple gazed over it.
Spiders tiptoe around their lacy cobwebs
Waiting for the break of day.
Fox cubs huddle together on mossy tree stumps
As badgers scuttle through the shadows.
The golden sun starts to rise over snowy mountains.
Night dies out.
The sun booms out as the moon yawns and drifts out of the way.
Cheeky blackbirds chirp at the old, sleepy cat.
The world shines like a lonely star giving its light to the earth.
The radiant daybreak is over.

Kathryn Armitage (10)
Hutton Rudby Primary School, Yarm

My Friend Alice

My friend Alice is very pretty,
She loves to sing and dance,
My friend Alice likes to talk,
I think she's rather good at it,
Alice adores her pony Mac,
He is a bit of a Macsweeny (weird),
My friend Alice is a great laugh,
I think she rather enjoys it,
Me and Alice are best friends,
We stick together like glue.

Grace Smeaton (10)
Hutton Rudby Primary School, Yarm

In The Early Hours Of The Morning

In the early hours of the morning,
The moon slowly fades away to make room for the sun,
The last glinting stars are like the lights in a house
When people are going to bed.
The sun coming over the cities ready for the break of day to come,
The moon slowly melts away over the top of the stunning mountains,
The silhouette of the old, gnarled oak tree,
Like a hand reaching out to grab something.
The lights of flats and houses slowly coming on one by one,
From the branches of the ancient conker tree,
A robin sings in the morning sun, then slowly flies away,
The blinding sun in the red sky moves slowly around the world
In the early hours of the morning.

Evie Mallinson (10)
Hutton Rudby Primary School, Yarm

Hours Of Awakening

As the morning slowly comes nearer
The stars start to fade
While the sun glows red, ready to light the sky.

Foxes go back to their dens where their mother awaits.
City lights go out one by one
As the first car drives on the deserted road.

The first fish is seen swimming gracefully in the dreamy lake.
The mountains' silhouettes gaze at the world below.
The sun creeps up behind the misty mountains to make a new day.

Keir Walker (10)
Hutton Rudby Primary School, Yarm

A Winter Morning

I gaze out of my bedroom window and I see . . .
A shooting star filtering light through old, battered trees.
I see a family of foxes tiptoe silently into a warm den.
I see reflections of grey turn to a golden-red.
I see a golden retriever stream down an early morning beach.
I see frozen lilies float on a dark, twinkling lake.
I see street lamps slowly dim in a dusky background.
I see the first blackbird stir in the cool twilight morning.
I see velvet, violet, silver clouds in a new sun setting.

Robbie Quigley (10)
Hutton Rudby Primary School, Yarm

World's First Breath

I'm glad it's the night.
In the cold darkness the moon's first rays cascade down
Like shining blades whirling down to the jet-black world below.
The badgers slide silently away to their snug warm dens for the day,
Their matted fur brushing the crusty earth below as the day breaks.
The first sunlight sauntering down the steps of the sky,
The crimson brightness shadows the mountain
Making an ebbing light over the world.
I'm glad it's day.

Hugh McNeela (10)
Hutton Rudby Primary School, Yarm

My Class!

Hugh and George are like identical twins, they always love to talk
And Mr Robinson perched and peering, observing like a hawk.
Mrs Hoyle is always walking round and well Tom . . . he just frowned.
Jessica absolutely adores to sing
Grace loves horses (totally mad)
And always after school, she goes riding.

Rosie Holmes (10)
Hutton Rudby Primary School, Yarm

Ode To Autumn

Hast thou smelt the elegant scent of the roses?
The stubble is weeping as thou slice the corn
Yonder spindly spiders catch flies in their webs
Hast thou seen the crispy leaves spiral down
To the hard, frosty ground?

Thou old weeping oak tree sways from side to side
Keeping itself warm,
Hast thou noticed the changes in the sky?
Has thou noticed the hedgehogs hibernating
For the cold winter months?

Holly Wilkinson (10)
Hutton Rudby Primary School, Yarm

Football Madness

F ootball crazy
O ffsides are drool
O ut goes the ball
T hrow in comes in the box
B all to Shearer
A cracking, cracking goal!
L aughing and cheering
L oving the game.

Christopher McDonald (10)
Lukes Lane Community Primary School, Hebburn

Autumn Poem

One sunshiny day, I looked up to the sky
The sun glazed in my eyes.
I could see the clouds slowly flowing across the light, bright, blue sky.
I heard trees swaying in the cold, calm breeze
I could smell the sweet smell of dinners being made.

Katie McBarron & Natasha Rowell (9)
Lukes Lane Community Primary School, Hebburn

Beginning Of Autumn

The tall trees are blown by the soft, breezy wind
The lovely green grass scattered in the brown, crunchy leaves
As the magpies are tweeting away
The bugs crawl and flying up to tall trees.
Children coming out to play.
They're playing here, playing there, playing everywhere.
They're jumping up, jumping down
They're jumping on the damp, crunchy ground
The bell has rung it's time to go
Everyone walks to the class, very slow.

Peter Braithwaite (9)
Lukes Lane Community Primary School, Hebburn

The Playtime Song

Watch out everyone, they've left their home,
Pushing, screaming, playtime's come,
Skipping, running, all around.
Out the school, onto the ground,
Children falling into the grass
Children running at mass,
The bell has rung, it's time to go,
They all have run and now they're slow.

Nathan Bull (9)
Lukes Lane Community Primary School, Hebburn

Autumn

One morning I felt the breeze dancing lightly across my face
I could hear leaves fluttering down from the tall trees
I could feel the leaves crackling under my damp feet.
I heard acorn cups falling off trees onto the ground.
Squirrels jumping tree to tree, trying to find a new home.
I could see grasshoppers jumping so high
It looked like they were in the sky.

Josh Wright (9)
Lukes Lane Community Primary School, Hebburn

Autumn Breeze

I looked out of my window and saw the spectacular clouds.
They were so slowly passing me.
I looked up so high that I got a flash in my eye.
The flash shocked me and I fell back.
When I woke up the sun shone
And it looked like the world.
In the playground there are some flowers that grow every day.
If you look at them, you feel like they're singing to you.
If you look through the fence you can see the empty fields.

Rebeka Pyle (8)
Lukes Lane Community Primary School, Hebburn

The Different Kind Of Objects

As I walked around the playground
There was a flash of sun on the yard
The window was open and the breeze came in,
It dances around the tables.
The van went around
The sound was really noisy when it reverses.
The pink and blue flowers danced around the wind
The tree swished around
The leaves dropped down and turned red.

Bethany Hearst (8)
Lukes Lane Community Primary School, Hebburn

Autumn Poem

One morning I felt the breeze dancing lightly across my face
I could hear leaves fluttering down from the tall trees.
I could feel the leaves crackling under my damp feet.
I heard an acorn cup falling off the trees onto the ground.
Squirrels jumping from tree to tree trying to find a new home.
A could see grasshoppers jumping so high
It looked like they're in the sky.

David Aplin (8)
Lukes Lane Community Primary School, Hebburn

My Wonderful School

Flowers and bushes swaying gently in the breeze
To the birds' beautiful song.
I turned round and saw a flash of light,
Right on the strike of midday.
Rough people bash walls next to shining red doors
Juicy berries fade through the soft breezy wind
Tiny, scuttling insects crawling all around,
Insects flying off and onto the ground.

Kenneth Liddle (8)
Lukes Lane Community Primary School, Hebburn

The Brightness In Lukes Lane School

The lone trees sway as the wind blows,
The beautiful flowerbeds are full of gorgeous flowers
As you stand on the twigs you can feel them in your shoes.
The blueberries are poisonous, never eat them.
Pretty colours all around wherever you look
Colours all around, even on the playground.
The chestnut trees, as you walk around the conkers are all around.

Emily Malone & Kate Kenyon (8)
Lukes Lane Community Primary School, Hebburn

Football Madness

F ootball crazy
O ffsides are drool
O ut goes the ball
T hrow in comes
B all to Shearer
A cracking, cracking goal!
L aughing and cheering
L oving the game.

Jack Howorth (10)
Lukes Lane Community Primary School, Hebburn

Hallowe'en

H ats, masks and costumes
A little boy cries
L eaving houses to visit others
L ovely sweets and treats
O range pumpkins glow
W indows lit by candlelight
E verybody runs for the sweets
E veryone runs around the streets
N ow the end of Hallowe'en has come, bye till next year.

Kyle Hudson (10)
Lukes Lane Community Primary School, Hebburn

Hallowe'en

H ats, masks and costumes
A lways trick or treat
L ovely sweets and other stuff
L eaving houses to go to another
O range pumpkins glow
W indows lit by candlelight
E veryone gives us frights
E veryone runs around the streets
N ow Hallowe'en has gone, see you all next year.

Liam Growcott (10)
Lukes Lane Community Primary School, Hebburn

Autumn

A sunny time of year
U nder the baring trees
T he leaves turn red, yellow and orange
U nder the warm sun
M any animals approaching winter's chill
N ice memories, soon to fade.

Courtney Sinclair (10)
Lukes Lane Community Primary School, Hebburn

Hallowe'en

H aunted house
A live with zombies walking around
L iving dead awakes
L urking black cats in the moonlight
O wls hooting
W arning ghosts to keep away
E vil awaks
E nter the dead
N ear the graveyard zombies walk.

Shannon Hays & Athena Daley (10)
Lukes Lane Community Primary School, Hebburn

New Baby

N appies filled with poo
E ndless crying too
W hile I'm asleep she's awake.

B aby, oh goodness sake
A really moody girl
B ut the best in the world
Y ou'll never love her as much as me.

Kyl Drummond (10)
Lukes Lane Community Primary School, Hebburn

Hallowe'en Night

H allowe'en night
A lways creepy
L it lanterns glowing
L ights on in houses
O ne long year
W itches flying around on broomsticks
E nter the zombies
E vil skeletons jiggling about
N ever-ending night!

Sharlott Sherwin (10)
Lukes Lane Community Primary School, Hebburn

Hallowe'en

H allowe'en
A creepy night
L ong night
L ate night
O ne night in a year
W itches flying and cackling
E ternal ghost
E vil devil
N ever-ending fright.

Emily Surrey (10)
Lukes Lane Community Primary School, Hebburn

Ice Melting

I ce
C ube
E xperiment

M elting
E xciting science
L ooking in
T hawing
I cy snow
N ice ice
G ood ice.

Keiran Percy (8)
Lukes Lane Community Primary School, Hebburn

If

If the trees were made of lollipops
And the ground was made of sugar sweets
If the fences were made of candy sticks
And the lakes were made of custard
Then what would we have to drink?

Natasha Wright (11)
Lukes Lane Community Primary School, Hebburn

Hallowe'en

H allowe'en is so much fun
A lot of children dressing up
L eaving houses with their sweets
L ots of frightening Hallowe'en costumes
O nly happens once a year
W atch out, there are lots of ghosts, vampires and gremlins around
E verywhere babies crying
E very time you knock on a door
N ever leave your mum's side or else!

Hannah Hearst (10)
Lukes Lane Community Primary School, Hebburn

Ice Melting

I ce cubes
C old
E xperiment

M elting ice
E xciting
L aughing people
T emperature
I ce-cold
N ice
G littering ice.

Emma Porter (7)
Lukes Lane Community Primary School, Hebburn

If

If the lamp posts were lollipops
And if footballs were chocolate
And leaves were crisps
And if water was melted chocolate
And fences were candy sticks
Then how would we stay healthy?

Mark Marshall (10)
Lukes Lane Community Primary School, Hebburn

Keeping Cold

K ids working
E xcellent
E xperiment
P lastic cups
I ce
N ice ice
G etting warm

C old ice
O h ice
L isten carefully
D rip, drip!

Paige Burn (8)
Lukes Lane Community Primary School, Hebburn

Keeping Cold

K ids looking
E xcellent
E xperiment
P eeping eyes, watching
I ce-cold
N oise, ice cracking, ice
G lass ice

C old drops of water
O ld ice still melting
L ooking at ice
D ripping ice.

Carley Gray (9)
Lukes Lane Community Primary School, Hebburn

Keeping Cool

K eeping cold
E xperiment
E xplore
P lastic cups
I ce
N ice ice
G ood experiment

C lear white
O oh ice
L ukes Lane school
D rip-drop, drip-drop!

Lucy Aplin (7)
Lukes Lane Community Primary School, Hebburn

Ice Melting

I ce cubes
C old, cold, cold
E xperiments are good.

M elting ice cubes
E xtremely hard
L ooking carefully
T emperature rising
I ce in a cup
N ice ice
G iggling teacher.

Emma Sherwin (8)
Lukes Lane Community Primary School, Hebburn

Keeping Cold

K eeping cold
E xciting
E xperiment
P lop, plop, plop
I ce cubes
N ice cubes
G littering ice

C old, cold, cold
O ld ice
L earning science
D rip, drip!

Alysha Walton (8)
Lukes Lane Community Primary School, Hebburn

Ice Melting

I ce
C ubes
E xperiment

M elting
E xcellent science
L isten carefully
T able top experiment
I ce watching
N ice ice
G etting smaller.

Abbie Butler (8)
Lukes Lane Community Primary School, Hebburn

Ice Melting

I ce
C hilly
E xperiment

M elting
E xtreme experiment
L istening
T emperature
I ce-cold
N ice ice
G littering ice.

Jessica Scott (8)
Lukes Lane Community Primary School, Hebburn

Ice Melting

I ce cube
C old, cold, cold
E xperiment

M elting ice
E xtremely hard
L ook at the ice cubes
T emperature is cold
I like ice cubes
N ice ice
G rowing temperature.

Chelsea McMahon (8)
Lukes Lane Community Primary School, Hebburn

Keeping Cool

I ce forming
C old and square
E xtremely hard

C lear and wet
U ntil it melts
B ig or small
E xperiment over
S lips away.

Chloe Aisbitt, Robert Goldburn, Kristopher McGeary (7) & Craig Smith (8)
Lukes Lane Community Primary School, Hebburn

School Dinners

I hate school dinners,
Sloppy mash covered in gravy!
And for dessert it's worse
Rotten apples and oranges.

Would you eat it?
Sloppy mash and rotten apples!
Well, I'm glad to tell you that
I have packed lunches.

Eran Cotterill (8)
Markland Hill CP School, Bolton

The Sea

The ocean is blue, the sand is yellow
The fish are in caves at night
The sharks are out for a bite
And the ships go off to set sail
The funnels go toot
And all the men wave goodbye.

Elliott Kilshaw (9)
Markland Hill CP School, Bolton

The Scrapyard

A giant steel fist came crashing down and knocked out the windows;
Suddenly a huge hammer swung down, kicked the car on the rear
Causing it to shudder forward;
A giant magnetic cylinder on the roof picked it up then dropped it;
Suddenly big jets of flame came, flaring out,
Lapping the sides of the car, softening the metal;
Then the walls started to close in squeezing the car into a cube!

Tom Gorman (9)
Markland Hill CP School, Bolton

The Utility Room

In the new shiny utility room,
the Hoover shouted,
the dryer screamed,
the washing machine jumped,
the freezer and fridge shivered,
the door shone,
the wall sparkled,
the floor gleamed
and everything was *noisy!*

Femi Nylander (9)
Markland Hill CP School, Bolton

Love

Love is light red
Love smells like a tulip
It looks like a heart of gold
Love feels like a bunch of roses
It sounds like a pot of lips
Love lives in a princess castle.

Megan Halsall (7)
Markland Hill CP School, Bolton

Fireworks

Spirals spinning with the wind
The wheel sulked, while people grinned
The other fireworks are free
While one is nailed to a tree.

My dad crouches holding a taper
As he lights the blue touch paper
The rocket zooms into the night
Then explodes in a shower of light.

People look up in excitement and wonder
Then a crash and a rumble like thunder
The sparks are over, now it dies
Softly to the ground it flies.

Simon Hind (8)
Markland Hill CP School, Bolton

Love

Love is bright red like our heart
Love smells like bright red strawberries
It looks like a huge, big rainbow
Love feels like lovely bright roses
It sounds like the sun rising up
Love lives inside us.

Lina Bukhari (7)
Markland Hill CP School, Bolton

The Rocket

I love Bonfire Night
The rocket goes filling up the sky
The cartwheel spins fast a lot lower down
I just love Bonfire Night.

Ryan Cadman (9)
Markland Hill CP School, Bolton

In The Playground

You'll never hear anything but . . .
'Miss, Miss, he did this and she did that.'
People on duty must get sick of it,
Boys shouting, 'What a goal!' as they score,
Girls fighting as they play,
Go to the teacher and complain,
Need the toilet, need a drink,
Go round the corner and knock at the door,
Never mess and be quick,
Get your coat before you come out
And don't keep running in and out,
Go to the teacher because you've fallen over,
What a bang!

Chloe Smith (8)
Markland Hill CP School, Bolton

Joy

Joy is shiny blue
Joy smells like fresh apples
It looks like someone happy
Joy feels like a soft dog
It sounds like the birds singing
Joy lives in your heart.

Callum Rout (7)
Markland Hill CP School, Bolton

War

War is dark black
War smells like rotten soldiers
It looks like smoky-black
War feels like darkness
It sounds like guns firing
War lives in a ghost town.

Eleanor Schenk (7)
Markland Hill CP School, Bolton

Under and Over

Under the water, over the land
Children playing on the sand.
Fishes swimming in the sea,
Shouting to fishermen, 'You can't catch me!'
Under the water, over the land
Adults sunbathing to get a tan
Children hiding to get some shade!
Fishermen shouting, 'I caught 'er!'
Fish squirming in hand!

Jaya Entwistle (8)
Markland Hill CP School, Bolton

Rainbow Colours

Red, yellow, pink and green
The prettiest colours I've ever seen
Orange, purple, black and blue
How about you?
Is it white or indigo?
What other colours do you know?
Red, yellow, pink and green
The prettiest colours I've even seen!

Samantha Yates (9)
Markland Hill CP School, Bolton

War

War is the time when people die
War is the time when children cry
Every day, every night
Pray for them,
Hope they don't die.

Louis Hall-Dunleavy (7)
Markland Hill CP School, Bolton

Night

Night is a dangerous fellow, he is dark and gloomy,
He makes me feel frightened and scared,
His face looks scary and frightening in his stare,
His eyes are blood-red and flaming hot,
His mouth is just a dark pit with no light coming in,
Lips black and wrinkled
His hair is long, dark and black,
His clothes are made of dark black lining, all ripped and cut,
When he moves he floats through the air
He lives in a dark, dark castle with his friend Nightmare
And it is never quite there!
Night scares me!

Jonathon Bradley (10)
Markland Hill CP School, Bolton

Love

Love is shimmering pink
Love smells like lavender
It looks like a love heart
Love feels like a smooth rabbit
It sounds like kisses
Love lives in a prince.

Scott Corrigan (7)
Markland Hill CP School, Bolton

Teddy Bears

Cuddly teddy bears are not hard
Like remote controlled racing cars
It is cuddly for sleeping with at night
Cuddly teddy bears cannot walk
Like a human being, like us.

Jack Dawson (7)
Markland Hill CP School, Bolton

Love

Love is light red
Love smells like Michaelmas daisies
It looks like a white dove
Love feels like a smooth hamster
It sounds like a heart beating
Love lives in a heart.

Christopher McEvoy (7)
Markland Hill CP School, Bolton

Love

Love is light red
Love smells like fresh roses in the air
It looks like stars floating around in the sky
Love feels like soft cushions
Love sounds like someone's heart beating slowly
It lives in a big shimmering glass princess.

Niamh Bolton (7)
Markland Hill CP School, Bolton

Love

Love is bright red
Love smells like beautiful roses
It looks like bright red tulips
Love feels like silk
It sounds like birds singing
Love lives in people's hearts.

Jennifer Walmsley (7)
Markland Hill CP School, Bolton

Love

Love is light pink.
It smells like perfume.
It looks like a lovely rose.
Love feels like soft material.
Love is everywhere.
It lives in light green grass.

Olivia Milne (7)
Markland Hill CP School, Bolton

Happiness

Happiness is bright pink
Happiness smells like fresh roses
It looks like children playing
Happiness feels like people hugging you
It sounds like twinkling fairies
Happiness lives in the heart of a child.

Lucy Entwistle (7)
Markland Hill CP School, Bolton

Bears

Bears are big, bears are small
Bears are tall, bears play ball
Bears are cuddly, bears are fluffy
Bears eat honey
Yum-yum for my tum.

Julia E Sabery (7)
Markland Hill CP School, Bolton

Joy

Joy is light blue.
Joy smells like chocolate.
It looks like love.
Joy feels like caring.
It sounds like a heart beating.
It lives in our heart.

Nathan Dhodakia (7)
Markland Hill CP School, Bolton

War

War is dark black
War smells like a rotten frog
It looks like a horrid army
War feels like sadness
It sounds like howling ghosts
War lives in the heart of a devil.

Kate Barnett (7)
Markland Hill CP School, Bolton

War

War is very dark
War smells like rotten carrots
It looks like death
War feels like hate
It sounds like a screaming mother
War lives in the heart of a ghost.

Fergus Plant (7)
Markland Hill CP School, Bolton

Joy

Joy is purple and full of hope.
Joy smells like perfume.
It looks like lovely curls.
Joy feels soft and smooth.
It sounds like children singing.
Joy lives in your heart.

Anya Cotterill (7)
Markland Hill CP School, Bolton

Animals

Animals in the zoo
Lions growling and prowling
Monkeys jumping and swinging
Snakes slithering up and down
Some are poisonous
Horses galloping in the field.

Ryan Roocroft (9)
Markland Hill CP School, Bolton

Love

Love is light green.
Love smells like a bunch of flowers.
It looks like a love heart.
Love feels like a smooth flower.
It sounds like a rabbit.
Love lives in a princess.

Bradley Light (7)
Markland Hill CP School, Bolton

Dark

Night,
gentle, but clutches tight,
the noises, blood-curdling
but the darkness soothing.

Dark glides round your room at night,
makes you think of your doom tonight,
but the longer you endure,
dark becomes more secure.

Not a single feature missed,
dark's face a gentle mist,
a faint blue frown forms the mouth,
eyes tinted red, facing south.

Hair framing dark face with smoke,
then to me the dark spoke,
no more than a whisper in my ear,
yet the voice rang out true and clear.

Dark swarms in, soon as light goes out,
he lives there till dawn comes about,
whether night wraps you up or makes you think of one who died,
now you can run but you can't hide!

Tessa Darbishire (10)
Markland Hill CP School, Bolton

Agents

The MI6 agents
Going on a mission,
Reading a comic on the way,
Wanting the next edition.
In the building, sneaking through a vent,
Then I just remember I hadn't paid the rent.
Taking out guards with my M9 gun,
Thinking to myself, *oh this is fun.*

Joseph Barton (10)
Markland Hill CP School, Bolton

Night

Night is an evil, but beautiful girl,
She's heartless and cruel, her skin white as pearl
She lives in a castle with her cat until dark
She gives children dreams to make their toes curl.
You wonder while sleeping, you've had a scare,
How would you like to know what she wears?

Her black silk-cut dress, is woven by ghouls,
Who get their silk from Hell,
Her never-ending dress is the evil, dark night,
She's wicked and nasty, extremely cruel
You wonder while sleeping, you've had a scare
Now would you like to know about her hair?

Like black silk woven by angels in the clouds
All goodness and light her hair enshrouds
Into mist and swoops back to
Her castle on the moon.
Those sweet angels so feminine and kind
Until comes the night, in her horrible bind.

Her lips black as coal like Dracula's wives,
Her nails bloodstained red, like horrible knives,
Could slit your throat at once
Her eyes are the deepest blue,
Like an angry ocean on a stormy night.

So now you know your death sentence,
Is all the cause of 'her'
That evil, dark lady, in the castle
You'll soon get to meet that cruel girl
You wonder while sleeping, you've had a fright
But it's only the most evil, most terrible . . .
Night!

Katharine Horrocks (10)
Markland Hill CP School, Bolton

Can't . . . Late

Got up in the morning,
Bed moaned to me,
'You need more sleep,'
'Can't . . . late.'

Ran down to the kitchen,
Toast shouted to me,
'You need more toast,'
'Can't . . . late.'

Raced out to the car,
Car grunted to me,
'I desperately need oil,'
'Can't . . . late.'

Climbed into the car,
Shoes breathed to me,
'I need to be tied,'
'Can't . . . late.'

Finally got to work,
I stumbled out of the car,
Tripped over my shoelace,
Now I'm late even more!

My heart started pounding
I heard a blood-curdling scream,
I was sweating all over,
Then it happened!

I hate the night!

Catriona McLaughlin (10)
Markland Hill CP School, Bolton

Animal Alphabet

A is for ape, who scratches its armpit,
B is for bee, who buzzes all day,
C is for cat, who scales the rooftop,
D is for dog who's man's best friend,
E is for elephant, with a very long trunk,
F is for fly, who flies all day,
G is for gorilla, strong as a lion,
H is for hippopotamus, wallowing in the mud,
I is for iguana, clinging onto a tree,
J is for jaguar, running over the plains,
K is for koala bear, sitting under a tree,
L is for leopard, lying in the tree,
M is for mouse, who squeaks all night,
N is for newt, darting through the water,
O is for ostrich with a very long neck,
P is for python, sneaking through the grass,
Q is for queen bee, that sits and waits,
R is for rhino with one big horn,
S is for shark, who slides through the water,
T is for tiger, well camouflaged, ready to jump,
U is for unicorn, a mythical beast,
V is for viper, biting its victim,
W is for whale, swimming in the ocean,
X is for X-ray fish, glowing in the sea,
Y is for yellow dart frog, waiting in a pond,
Z is for zebra, escaping from lions.

John Yearsley (10)
Markland Hill CP School, Bolton

Night

Night is a neighbourly person who soothes you to sleep.

I dream something bad is going to happen then he comes
and drops me through something deep.
Later on I see his face, his eyes are blue, lips are light pink,
his hair is brown and he wears a suit.
One minute he is there, the next he is gone.

Surprised I am, then he is there on a mountain.

Suddenly he is next to me again.
He is so fast, he stops in front of me, I touch his face.
It is so soft, he walks over to a table so quiet.
He's drawing a picture . . . a house . . . on the moon.
Then he draws some more, he says he lives everywhere.
He points to the moon and says, 'Real home.'
Then he starts to float towards the moon,
His final word is, 'Goodnight.'

Oliver Halliwell (10)
Markland Hill CP School, Bolton

The Posh Cat

The posh cat
yawning loudly,
strolling slowly to the wall,
black and grey,
short and slim,
soft and silky skin,
goes to sleep, anywhere will do.

That is all about my cat.

Antony Evitts (8)
Markland Hill CP School, Bolton

Night

Night is a shadowy figure,
Floating eerily around me,
Staring with red, lifeless eyes,
Then he floats on silently.

His black rags trail on the floor,
They are ripped at the seams,
Night turns round to stare at me,
And in the moonlight his eyes gleam.

His mouth is stubborn and tight-lipped,
His hair is messy and black,
He takes one last look at me
And then he turns his back.

As he wanders on,
The dark begins to go,
I'll never forget that scary face
That was as white as snow.

Jack Wilson (10)
Markland Hill CP School, Bolton

I See A Black Cat

Stalking in the dark night.
She's crawling stealthily
In the shadow of a black car.
She's got a sly, cunning, black colour.
She has a thin and straight body.
The fur is as soft as it can be.
She makes a quiet purr when
She's in the mood to catch something.
She sleeps in her basket
Before she has her dinner.
Cats turn out to be fantastic pets.

Timothy Sinclair (8)
Markland Hill CP School, Bolton

Liquorice

I see a fat black cat.
It's sleeping on my green grass.
It's strolling very slowly.
It's dark, black like liquorice.
It's round and fat.
Its fur is very silky.
It makes a purring noise.
It sleeps and eats.
It is a very hungry cat.

Victoria Aspinall (8)
Markland Hill CP School, Bolton

Summer

Summer is great,
I am never late
for anything.
I'm always ready for a sing.

I like the summer breeze,
we're going to the park, not again!
My mum's forgotten the keys,
I like to swing,
I always sing.

Gemma Butterworth (10)
Markland Hill CP School, Bolton

Dinners

D inners are horrible, they stink out the place,
I hate school dinners.
N o one will return if you eat dinners,
N ice dinner ladies are normal, some are, some are not,
E xtra loud dinner ladies, quiet dinner ladies,
R ed food, lots of different colours, don't know what they are,
S ick, sick, 'Mum, don't make me eat school dinners!'

Sam Tempest (10)
Markland Hill CP School, Bolton

Liquorice

I see a black cat
purring and stretching,
stretching and walking.
Black and greyish,
short and thin,
big and furry.
'Miaow, miaow,'
Sleeps, eats and drinks,
the cat's gone to sleep.

Jack Hobson (7)
Markland Hill CP School, Bolton

Untitled

I see a black cat
lying on her owner's lap.
She's walking very poshly.
She is black and white,
Furry and thin.
'Miaow!' Sleeps, walks,
Purrs and scratches.
Cats are so furry.

Daniel Cramer (7)
Markland Hill CP School, Bolton

Cuddly Cats

I see a cat,
chasing a rat,
scorching Ginger,
tall and slim,
ginger and spiky
purring in the sun,
sleeps in the car,
miaows!

Andrew Catterall (8)
Markland Hill CP School, Bolton

Seasons Change

S ummer is hot,
E venings last so long,
A utumn is cold and wet,
S ometimes it is hot.
O n top of everything else, in winter you get snow,
N othing else can say it better,
S easons change.

C hristmas is in winter although it never snows,
H owever the weather, the world will still turn,
A nd I've chosen my favourite, so what's yours?
'N onsense,' I hear you shout, 'I hate them all.'
'G et out of town, they help us survive, you love them.'
E veryone shout, *'Seasons change!'*

Rowan Jade Starkie (10)
Markland Hill CP School, Bolton

Night

Night is a dreadful thing,
His hair is spiky black and blue,
His clothes are made of dark blue snakeskin,
His mouth is big, dark blue, with a long black tongue,
His face is spiky and scary, it's terrible,
His eyes are dark red in the shape of cats' eyes.
When he moves, he does it silently and swiftly,
When he speaks, it's always in a dark voice.
He makes me feel scared and cowardly,
He lives in a tunnel with no light and rats all around.

All I can say is, night scares me!

Jack Cumisky (11)
Markland Hill CP School, Bolton

I'd Like To Live In A Library

I'd like to live in a library where
the books come to life,
the rainbow shines and the apples are ripe,
while the sun is playing a fife.

I'd like to live in a jungle where
the grass kisses the trees, the sun is smiling,
the clouds are whining
and the honey is made by the bees.

I'd like to live in a forest where
the trees all mimic and moan,
the leaves are dancing across the path,
the river is starting to groan.

I'd like to live in a haunted house where
the ghost and ghouls shout, 'Woo!'
But that would freak me out a little,
would that freak you out too?

Nicole Turton (9)
Markland Hill CP School, Bolton

Rain

Angry clouds float high in the sky,
Oh no, they've begun to cry,
Raindrops fall down on the passer-by,
People rush to stay dry.

Raindrops dance on the windowpane,
Drawing pictures on the clear frame,
Drip, drip onto the ground,
Making puddles to splash around.

The sun jumps from behind the clouds,
Along with the rainbow with a coat of colours,
It won't be long till it arrives again.

Humayrah Natha (9)
Markland Hill CP School, Bolton

Night

Night is a nasty, dreadful thing, blood-curdling, horrifying.
He makes me feel scared and gives me nightmares.
His face is black,
His eyes are red and glow up in the pitch-blackness of the room,
His mouth is a big hole which sucks all the happiness out of you,
His hair is shiny grey,
His clothes are made of black silk.
When he moves, he glides through the air,
When he speaks, he makes you feel cold inside
He lives in the sky in the day until dark
And then he will come again.

Joshua A Sabery (10)
Markland Hill CP School, Bolton

Playful

I see a baby kitten
Playing with a ball,
Moving side to side.
White, soft kitten,
Delicate, cuddly ball,
Smooth white fur,
Purring to sleep,
Sleeping everywhere,
Magnificent cuddly ball.

Ellie McGivern (7)
Markland Hill CP School, Bolton

Night

Night is carer, a lover, something you can't get rid of
He makes me feel invulnerable, untouchable
His face looks gentle, mysterious and unidentified
His eyes are shiny blue, like a train coming out of a tunnel
His mouth is a charmer from darkness, like roses
His golden hair shines with a gleam
His clothes are made of blackness which covers the world
When he moves, he drifts in the sky just like a feather
When he speaks, his voice drifts you to a different land
He lives in a hole with nothing and completely nothing
Me, night and everything.

Giordano Calcatera (10)
Markland Hill CP School, Bolton

Cats

I see
a black cat
sitting near
the road,
sprinting as fast
as a car,
as black as
the sky at night,
as thin as
a paintbrush, and
as soft as
a teddy bear.
It makes a purring sound
and comes to cuddle you
and miaows a lot.

Joseph Agate (8)
Markland Hill CP School, Bolton

Seasons

Spring

Spring swooped down
and licked her flowers,
she swooped with summer
and they both danced together.

Summer

Summer swam in her warm air
and glided through her flowers
and spring and summer
went to find autumn.

Autumn

Autumn flew round and
looked after her flowers and trees,
and spring, summer and autumn
went to find winter.

Winter

Winter was diving through her snow and enjoying it.
Winter is best of all.
Spring, summer, autumn and winter
played with their seasons.

Ellie Gittins (9)
Markland Hill CP School, Bolton

Cats

I see a mean cat
purring for prey,
stalking away,
coal-black, round, fat,
golden fur,
purring sound.
It scrambles away.
I like this cat.

Jaimie Booth (8)
Markland Hill CP School, Bolton

Animals

Flying bats
Black cats
Slimy snails
Blue whales

Furry dogs
Jumping frogs
Funny bugs
Horrible slugs

Big hippo
Massive rhino
Grizzly bear
Floppy eared hare

Long snake
Lazy drake
Goose
And moose

Scary shark
Dogs bark
Flying bats
Black cats.

Natalie Aspinall (11)
Markland Hill CP School, Bolton

Cats

I see a shy cat
Sleeping in his bed,
Black cat.
The cat has a round body,
The cat's skin of fur is nice and soft.
My cat purrs,
It likes playing with people.
I like my cat.

Kara Siddall (9)
Markland Hill CP School, Bolton

Night

Once I crawled into my cosy bed,
Clutching the covers tight,
And rested on the pillow my weary head,
In crawled the burglar, night.

Disguised in a veil,
And dressed in a cloak,
His outstretched hands, frail,
Disappearing in a wisp of smoke.

Darkness closed in all around me,
Gliding all around the room,
Night came to overpower thee,
Is it a nightmare or is it my doom?

Once I fell asleep at midnight,
Darkness still swirling all around,
I'm hoping for the first light,
I hope darkness would seep through the ground.

Once I crawled out of my cosy bed,
Thinking about last hour's fright,
Awakening my weary head,
Out crawled the burglar, night.

Connor Stanford (10)
Markland Hill CP School, Bolton

Cat

I see a sly cat
purring away,
stalking silently,
silky black,
round, fat,
puffy,
stomping loudly,
standing on delicate toes.
I like this cat.

Melissa Callow (8)
Markland Hill CP School, Bolton

Night

Night is scary and looks like a creep,
She makes little children wail and weep,
Night is horrid and scary, certainly not nice,
She doesn't even care when she haunts thrice.

Night is atrocious,
An evil spirit above,
Yes, not like a raven, in a safe haven,
Look out for her because that's what she is.

She lives in the middle of nowhere, in a cave somewhere,
Nobody to live with but she doesn't care,
As the sun goes down she floats over the land,
She touches the sky with her evil hand,
Suddenly everything goes dismal and dark,
Like inside the jaws of a hungry shark.

She floats through houses,
She speaks in cackles,
Red eyes with black middles, pursed lips that will soon laugh,
Then she laughs her evil laugh and it all begins.

Alexander Walmsley (10)
Markland Hill CP School, Bolton

Mike

I see a baby kitten
Stalking its prey,
Curving into a silky ball,
Grey and silky,
Cuddly and soft,
Smooth and delicate,
Purring like music,
Arches its back,
Magnificent!

Mary Axon-Smith (8)
Markland Hill CP School, Bolton

The Posh Cat

I see a brave, posh cat
licking its fur,
standing on its toes,
with golden ginger fur,
long and flat,
puffy and soft,
purring contentedly,
walking with its tail sticking up.
'Miaow!'

Callum Shaw (7)
Markland Hill CP School, Bolton

Wind, Oh Wind

The wind screamed and howled,
The lion roared and prowled,
Out came the postie, off blew his hat,
Out came the dog chasing the cat!

Jonathan Chapman (9)
Markland Hill CP School, Bolton

Cat

I see a ginger cat
curling up into a ball,
walking poshly,
ginger with black streaks,
round and long,
soft fur.
It likes yawning,
it loves sliding
along the wall,
I think.

Robert Swinton (8)
Markland Hill CP School, Bolton

A Cat Called Domino

I see a coloured creature
hiding away
dodging to places.
It is black and white,
round and chubby,
silky and cuddly.
It makes a purring noise,
goes behind a curtain.
It is a cat.

Toby Minion (8)
Markland Hill CP School, Bolton

Rain

Rain, it's everywhere,
Slapping on the windowpane.
Wetting all the washing,
Mum is always tame,
Please stop rain.
Oh no, it's raining.

Emma Wallwork (10)
Markland Hill CP School, Bolton

Teddy

I see a shiny cat,
It is lying down sleepily purring,
It is stalking its prey,
It is ginger,
It is tall and thin,
It is cuddly and fluffy,
It makes a miaowing noise,
It sleeps anywhere,
It is a *magnificent cat!*

Alexandra Darbyshire (7)
Markland Hill CP School, Bolton

Cats

I see a furry cat
yawning loudly,
nodding away,
slate-black,
long and thin,
smooth and soft.
A screaming noise.
Sleeps on top of a piano.
It is called Cooper.
Miaow!

Muhammad Karim (8)
Markland Hill CP School, Bolton

The Haunted House

The spooks jiggle as the haunted house howls
The portraits follow you as you creep down the stairs
The owls hoot illuminated against the starry night
And the cupboards rattle with fear.

Amy Thorpe (9)
Markland Hill CP School, Bolton

The Tabby Cat

It sits on the window ledge,
It's a ginger cat,
It is a fat cat.
Its fur is soft,
It makes prowling noises.
It sleeps and lies down.
That is all about my cat.

Chloe Rothwell (7)
Markland Hill CP School, Bolton

The Storm

The black clouds fell over the town,
The raindrops jumped merrily on the windowpane,
The thunder suddenly roared as the clouds cried,
The lightning burst into a bright light and ran away,
The hailstones banged against the window,
The rain came back, merry with glee,
Then all of a sudden a brightness peered from behind a cloud,
The town was as hot as fire.

Chloe Bembridge (9)
Markland Hill CP School, Bolton

Cats

I see a furry cat purring away.
He gets up and scampers away,
He sees something else black like him.
The cat that we're talking about is quite thin
And his fur is soft, as soft as skin.
He growls at something, something strange,
It's just like he's reading a book,
But never turning the page.
Now this cat is called Cooper,
A really nice cat,
If you had him, then that's that!

Ben Lainé (8)
Markland Hill CP School, Bolton

Summer

Chicks begin to crawl and follow their mothers,
The summer sun caresses the earth with its beautiful beams,
The clouds float by like familiar faces,
Bubbles dancing above the grass,
The dew running off the lawn.

Emma Cavill (9)
Markland Hill CP School, Bolton

Bonfire Night

The fire spits, sparks everywhere
The fireworks shoot up and break like reaching fingers in the sky
The fireworks scream as they reach into the air
The sky changes its mind like someone dropping ink into water
Bang!
The colours jump out
Bang!
The light bulb lights the sky
Shhh, it's gone silent.

Eleanor Smith (9)
Markland Hill CP School, Bolton

The Fireworks

Fireworks scream and shout
One spins and dances
The others just run up to the sky
And explode in anger
Others dance and sing in the air
When they go up they talk
And laugh to each other
And then they blow up and shout
'Argh!'

Eve Thomasson (9)
Markland Hill CP School, Bolton

The Garden

The smiling and dancing sun hopped between
The marshmallow clouds.
The sad, grumpy pansies sitting in the corner.
The swaying grass green as green.
The big white fluffy marshmallows jumping up and down.
The bright, big sunflowers staring at the roses.
And there, standing still, was the big, kind house.

Katie Sutcliffe (9)
Markland Hill CP School, Bolton

Darkness Demon

I met at night the king of darkness,
He had a dreadful, frightening face,
His pitch-black gown glided across the floor,
I was sweating in dread because of the chilling sounds.

My eyes were tightly shut in fright,
His eyes were golden yellow with the glint of hatred,
But I heard only the slightest of sounds,
For it was the dreaded dark.

His mouth seemed bloodthirsty,
Full of fangs that had been used recently,
His tongue was black,
You could only just see, for it was so dark.

He had an evil, treacherous face,
Full of fear and anger,
His hair was pitch-black locks,
With a spirit holding grey hairband.

His clothes were long and trailing,
It was a dress made of dark silk,
The experience was horrifying,
It glided towards me in a menacing way.

Night steals your good dreams,
And replaces them with nightmares,
I am in this isolated domain every night,
Night is torture when you see him.

Jack Ward (10)
Markland Hill CP School, Bolton

Night

Night is the strangest thing,
along with his cat.
When you're asleep you can go anywhere,
just like that.

Your blanket could be a wetsuit,
so you could swim with the fish,
or you could be his cat at home
drinking from a dish.

Your bed could be a sailing boat,
or a hive with lots of bees.
Then you could go somewhere weird,
like a shop that sells French cheese.

Then night and his cat will go back home,
to their tree house in the park.
Then he'll give you more dreams again
when it gets dark.

Beth Fisher (10)
Markland Hill CP School, Bolton

Fire!

Fire, fire so, so bright
It gives me a big, big fright
As you watch it dance
It puts you in a trance.

The fire raged into the sky
And sparks flew everywhere.
Water approached as the enemy.
The fiery show is over.
Ember sleeps.

Robert Bury (9)
Markland Hill CP School, Bolton

In My House At Night

In my house at night,
everything is very different,
it's as if my toy cat will get up
and shake my hand.

In my house at night,
it's like all my clothes
will jump out of my wardrobe
and do the cancan.

In my house at night,
it's like my teapot will wake up
and make itself a cup of tea.

But that's all a dream,
Or is it?

Rebecca Caulfield (9)
Markland Hill CP School, Bolton

Sparks And Fire!

Sparks jumping in the fire,
Hot just like lava,
Running down a volcano,
All spurting out.

Fire is a different thing,
Burning down houses,
Jumping, dancing, shouting,
And hot just like the sun.

Ryan Boulton (9)
Markland Hill CP School, Bolton

The Weather

A storm strikes a peculiar light,
the hurricane runs, dances and sucks up shops,
the volcano shakes and spits out lava
for the sunshine has stopped.

Hailstone, sunshine, you're so fine,
you hammer on the window sill,
you strike our skin with your rays
and make us hot with your kindness.

Snow, snow you cover the world like a duvet,
you twirl around the sky and make us happy
every time you scatter on the ground with the wind.

Kellie Branagan (9)
Markland Hill CP School, Bolton

Night

Night is a hooded face that haunts you in your dreams,
You know it's there in your head when nothing's as it seems,
The room goes black, that's when it appears, when no one's
in the room,
You open your eyes, awakening with fright, nothing there but gloom,
Night surrounds you deep and black, making pictures in your head,
She whispers to you as you sleep, haunts you in your bed,
She's lonely, forsaken to most people's dreams yet still she haunts me,
She won't go away, she never leaves, I wish she would see what I see.

Beth Isherwood (10)
Markland Hill CP School, Bolton

Seasons

Spring

Flowers dancing in the sun on the hillside,
Chocolate eggs sitting on a wide and narrow window sill,
Buds peeping, seeing a bright and happy world.

Summer

The warm summer breeze kicked in after a chilly night,
Glossy green leaves swaying from a summery tree,
Cool shade from the trees shimmering on the forest floor.

Autumn

The windy day,
The countryside is a favourite place for walking,
Listen to the trees whispering and talking,
Look up and see sombre clouds appear to be running,
Walk through yellow daffodils waving and nodding,
Say goodbye to the disappearing face in the clouds,
Back to the noisy city and the big crowd.

Winter

The storm,
Rain running down the windowpane,
Thunder hitting the trees,
Lightning strikes the telephone wires,
Fences kicked over by the ghostly wind.

Bethany Coton (9)
Markland Hill CP School, Bolton

A Machine Factory

The soap machine blew bubbles,
While the chocolate machine was in all kinds of troubles.
The pottery machine staggered to a stop,
In the room that makes the pot.
The machine was on its back resting,
While the noise machine was making a terrible ring.
The sport machine was running with pace,
And the joke machine was putting a grin on the sad machine's face.
And over the factory machines were going crazy,
They all knew they were being lazy.
The noise machine was attempting to be clever,
But he had already had his chance,
The mood machine was in annoyance,
Every factory worker was in a trance.

Jonothan Kay (9)
Markland Hill CP School, Bolton

Alfie's Alien Spacecraft

Alfie's alien spacecraft
Jumps and jogs around
Alfie's alien spacecraft
Loves to chant and shout
Alfie's alien spacecraft
Hates to moan and groan
Alfie's alien spacecraft
Sucks up all the space dirt
To make planets clean.

Daniel Chapman (9)
Markland Hill CP School, Bolton

My Lava Lamp

Vision is cool and calm
But to the touch nips me with anger
So purple and white
Like essence of midnight
Or dawn fighting dusk with all their might.

Calls me to it with a creepy glance
Pulls me in with its delicate dance
Hugs my mind with its noxious charms
And sways around its graceful arms.

Outer space with asteroids moving at a slow pace
With every meteor winning the race
Check your lava lamp
Just in case.

Hannah Dagnall (9)
Markland Hill CP School, Bolton

The Storm

The rain was running down the windows,
The wind was howling through the trees.
The lightning hit the tree,
Along with the thunder roaring and rattling the windows.
As the village slept, nobody noticed the lightning
Bringing down the trees,
The animals scampered to get away from the dancing fire
From the tree that had caught fire.
The rain was eating the fire like a baby eating porridge.
When the storm finished a rainbow was stretching over the sky.

Matthew Lockyer (9)
Markland Hill CP School, Bolton

The Fire

The fire started in a fireplace,
Then suddenly the body started to grow and grow,
When the fire had eaten its way through the wall,
The hands of the flame began to flick and throw sparks everywhere,
The fire began to spread across the garden, and another and another.
It ate everything in its path.
The fire screeched all of a sudden because it had eaten a gas tank.
The fire ran to a field leaving everything burnt,
It spotted a defenceless little barn and glided across the grass,
The fire smiled menacingly as it ate the barn,
When it had eaten too much it screeched in pain and died.

Yasmin Aldcroft (9)
Markland Hill CP School, Bolton

My Aunt's Laundry

The washing machine screams and jigs,
it suddenly jerks its way forward slowly.

The tumble dryer bounces and jumps
in a very exciting fashion,
it halts to a stop then spits out clothes in every possible direction,
then sleeps.

The washing baskets wait,
standing by the door all in a line - one, two, three, four,
waiting to feed on next week's clothes.

Hannah Dagnall (9)
Markland Hill CP School, Bolton

The Fireworks

The fireworks scream as they enter the starry black sky.
It has hesitated, I wonder why?
Whizz, bang, boom, crash!
Boom, bang, cry, bash!
The rocket explodes and then the banger,
As the Roman candle jumps out with anger.
Red, yellow, green and blue,
They all fade together as the crowd goes, 'Ooooh!'
We all go home from the display,
Oh I wish I could jump and sing like the fireworks I saw today!

Samantha Bland (9)
Markland Hill CP School, Bolton

The Utility Room

In the new, shiny utility room,
the Hoover shouted,
the dryer screamed,
the washing machine jumped,
the freezer and fridge shivered,
the door shone,
the wall sparkled,
the floor gleamed
and everything was
noisy!

Femi Nylander (9)
Markland Hill CP School, Bolton

The Scrapyard

In a scrapyard where cars screech in pain
Yes, the dreaded crusher tucked well behind a wooden frame
Metal bars sit around
Waiting and waiting until they're found
A big, yellow sign hangs on the gate
Saying thieves will meet their fate
For what is waiting behind a mist of fog
Is a very vicious American dog
The whisper of rain starts to creep in
As it hammers on the cars it makes a din
The crusher is stopped by the thunder and rain
That has stopped cars being in pain.

Peter Walton (9)
Markland Hill CP School, Bolton

A Windy Forest

I went for a walk in the old, windy forest
When I got there I heard the leaves dancing across the floor
It was raining
The daisies rubbed shoulders as I walked through them
The clouds winked as the rain was falling
The trees waving backwards and forwards.

The wind skipped across the ground
The twigs hopped across the floor
I walked back home into the town
Where everything was loud and noisy.

Isaac Freudenberger (9)
Markland Hill CP School, Bolton

Night

Night is a nasty, foul, loathsome, lazy thing,
Night is a lonely, scary, creepy beast,
He's so forsaken and isolated,
He gives you nightmares you'll never forget,
Night is a burglar, an intruder,
His face is like a misty night creeping through your curtains,
He has dark brown eyes glowing in the dark,
He has a colossal, misty mouth,
His hair is wavy and black,
He has a jet-black, spooky cloak,
Night lives everywhere,
Night freaks you out!

Tom Johnston (10)
Markland Hill CP School, Bolton

Wild Fire

Lightning ran at the ground,
Fire jumped out of the earth,
It ran over to some trees,
Fire licked and watched trees faint,
The beautiful, bubbling brook ran away from the fire,
All the wild flowers sunk into the earth,
The fire destroyed the bridge,
Suddenly the flames were suffocating in the water,
As if by magic they disappeared,
Wild flowers popped out relieved to find no damage.

Caroline Hayes (9)
Markland Hill CP School, Bolton

Night

Night is a dark, friendly giant,
With light blue eyes and light brown hair.
His face is smiling and oh so caring,
Happy in his lonely space.

His robe is grand and fit for a king,
Coloured light brown and a shade of grey.
Fits into the background of precious night,
Where he will always stay.

His sandals are no ordinary sandals,
Reflecting the light of his friend the moon.
They are the only light things he ever wears,
And he will wear them for the rest of his days.

Ewan Smith (10)
Markland Hill CP School, Bolton

The Swamp

The big swamp
where the snail walks on one foot
the trees whispers in the breeze
the sun caresses the scary caves
they become clear
the caves are now divine
the rainbow of smells sweeps through the swamp
the pixies dance in the air
and the bats glide in the caves.

Ben Hitchen (9)
Markland Hill CP School, Bolton

Night

Night is kind and a calm place,
She makes me feel like I'm safe.
Her eyes are nice, kind and light blue,
Her mouth is like a cave but a secure kind of cave.

Her face looks like a loving face
That makes you think of nice dreams,
Her hair is like dark green grass and is as soft as leaves,
Her clothes are a mantle made from leaves and trees.

She moves like the wind, swiftly and silently,
She speaks like a caring grandma saying goodnight,
She lives in a place where no one's there,
It ends with just . . .
Night, her and me!

Isabelle Stokes (10)
Markland Hill CP School, Bolton

Night

Night is a kind, neighbourly spirit,
She has golden hair and light blue eyes,
Night likes to dance and never shout.

She makes me want to dance and sing,
For all the presents she would send,
She never wears white but only black.

But in the morning she becomes ghostly,
Ghostly, mean and horrid . . .

Louise Kennedy (10)
Markland Hill CP School, Bolton

Night

Night is a cloaked figure turning everything into darkness
He makes me feel cold, alone and scared
He wears an old black cloak wrapped around himself
His face is pale and lifeless
His eyes are blood-red with dark purple bags beneath
His lips are pursed together and are as white as snow
His hair is white and tousled
When he speaks the air becomes icy
When he moves his dark tail flutters and a frosty breeze follows
He lives in a black cave with bloodsucking bats
Night is a terrifying thing
Beware!

Megan Scott (10)
Markland Hill CP School, Bolton

Night

Night is a horrible experience which can't be forgotten
The piercing darkness makes me feel so insecure
That pale, ghostly face would scare the bravest man on Earth
Those terrifying black eyes staring at you during a nightmare
She creeps so subtly no one would realise
That hair of hers is very creepy
The colour ghostly grey which trails along the floor like a snake
The cold, murderous mouth is so scary it makes me sweat with fright
She lives in the gloom of darkness with subtle movements and caution
Her voice is so murderous it crackles every now and then
Night horrifies me!

Ayesha Munshi (10)
Markland Hill CP School, Bolton

Night - Good Or Bad?

Night, she is lovely, safe and warm,
Her hair is as blonde as harvest corn,
He is not lovely, safe or warm,
He'll try to attack you with his horns.

But she is so nice like a warm black coat,
And a loving, gentle voice as she makes her quote,
You will be safe all through the night,
In the morning I'll send down light.

Yes, but he's so lonely, dark and cold,
His eyes are like two black holes,
The bright eyed angel said I'd have no nightmares,
But I've got to remember the devil still stares.

Francesca Bury (10)
Markland Hill CP School, Bolton

Parents

P arents pick their noses and make sure nobody knows
A nd always pose to look a lot younger
R eading and writing they never shut up. Shouting and balling isn't their thing
E xtraordinary and weird they may be, they never stop shouting at me
N ice as they are I never want to change them as young as I am
T alented and funny, why do they act like a bunny?
S illy as they are I still love them, I wouldn't swap them for the world!

Thomas Kavanagh (10)
Markland Hill CP School, Bolton

Night

Night is a lovely man, he's warm and comfy,
He makes me feel safe and light-hearted,
His face looks mild and kindly,
His eyes are as red as rubies,
His mouth is small and smooth,
His hair as black as coal,
His clothes are made of silk and cotton,
When he moves you can feel the warmness,
When he speaks a cold shot runs down your spine,
He lives in an underground, shadowy cave with rivers, rocks
and night animals,
But night is with me.

Ryan Greenhalgh (10)
Markland Hill CP School, Bolton

Night

Night, it brings with it the foul stench of fear.
It is so lovely, it feels like all the feelings have been sucked dry.
He's so terrifying when he wanders through the mists.
It is like he's waiting for something.
He is not always frightening, most of the time he's stunning,
But when he's angry he can turn into a huge demon.
He terrifies people until they're sent to the land of dreams.
Night is his domain, his kingdom, but at first light of dawn
that all changes.
He falls into oblivion paralysed in the deepest caverns,
But next night he will hit back and hit back hard.

Sam Burthem (10)
Markland Hill CP School, Bolton

Night

Night is a scary, lonely place
He makes me frightened and uncomfortable
His face is dreadful, beastly and scary
His eyes are red with a touch of nastiness
Long, scraggy hair as black as coal
Clothes made of leather and rope wrapped round its waist
When it moves it leaves a trail of blood
His voice is croaky, he can hardly speak
He lives in a shack in the middle of the wood
I would stop dreaming if I could.

Rebecca Eccles (10)
Markland Hill CP School, Bolton

Anger - Haiku

Cruel, red, hot, steaming,
Burning up inside your head.
It explodes - bang! Bang!

Olivia Topham (10)
Newcastle Church High School, Newcastle-upon-Tyne

The Rainbow - Haiku

It's a masterpiece,
An arch of many colours,
Framing the grey sky.

Julia Purvis (10)
Newcastle Church High School, Newcastle-upon-Tyne

Rush Hour

I hear the roaring engine of a chic Ferrari whizzing by
Like a newly lit rocket which surges forth into the midnight sky.
There are noisy horns beeping like a fog horn
On a misty, grey island as the tide surrounds it, the water lashing.
I hear the windscreen wipers as the rain beats down heavily
Like a young child with a spanking new drum kit.
The loud, banging radio is ringing in my ears.
My father is bellowing expletives at the top of his voice
At the car alongside us, competing for space.
There are more fog horns - even a bus has thunderously joined in.
It's getting too much!
My head is aching, throbbing, thumping.
Thump! Thump! Thump!
I hear the piercing sound of a police siren with its bright blue light
Flashing - a sapphire glinting as it catches the morning sun.
My anxious heart is booming.
Faster, faster, faster . . .
It's motorway mayhem.
Beep, beep, screech . . . beeeep!
Crash!

Silence . . .
I scream loudly out of control,
My stomach fearfully churning
Like a cement mixer turning the cement.
Blood is smeared on the cracked windscreen,
Staining like red wine spilt on a pure white wedding dess.
I watch it merge with the raindrops.

I slowly drift to sleep . . .

Francesca Thornton (10)
Newcastle Church High School, Newcastle-upon-Tyne

Summer Sunshine

Screeching seagulls fill the air.
Waves crash into the rough rocks with a splash
That echoes in my ear.
Speedboats zoom past,
Roaring like hungry, untamed lions.

People dive in the azure waters
From jagged, wind-battered rocks
With a crash loud enough to be heard a mile away.
While children run like cheetahs
Kicking sand as they go.

The cash register in the shack
Repeatedly rings in my head.
The boy blubbers as his ice cream melts in the sand.
The frisbee whizzes by
With the buzzing of a bee collecting sweet nectar.

The gleeful dog runs for the bouncing ball
Like a torpedo.
The pitter-patter of the pebble skipping in the sea
Calms the soul.
I've seen the beach.
I will now paint its picture.

Katherine Andersen (10)
Newcastle Church High School, Newcastle-upon-Tyne

Life - Haiku

Life is a ladder
We climb, sometimes we fall off.
At our death it snaps.

Abigail Buchan (11)
Newcastle Church High School, Newcastle-upon-Tyne

War

A bang of a mortar sends the missile through the air;
The clatter of an angry machine gun makes its reply.
A bomb lighting the sky with fire as it *booms!*
Shrapnel falls to the trembling ground.
Hundreds of German aeroplanes can be seen,
They are like black menacing birds patrolling the sky.

Houses shudder violently with the deafening noise.
They have been hit by a big, dirty bomb.
The people crawl helplessly out of the crumbling buildings,
Years of work destroyed in seconds.
People crying with fear as the war unfolds,
Louder, louder, louder.

Sergeants commanding orders.
The voices of lost children.
The sirens of the air raid shelters,
Fill the air.

Stillness

Gunfire has ended.
Black smoke smothers the sky,
Dust falls to the earth very gently, quietly.
There are no houses left,
It is all just rubble.

Henrietta Price (11)
Newcastle Church High School, Newcastle-upon-Tyne

Anger

Anger is like the smell of smoke.
Anger is like the high-pitched screaming in my ears.
Anger is like the sound of explosions in my ears.
Anger is a boiling hot chilli that burns through your tongue.
Anger is the taste of dripping wet blood.
Anger is like a hole of pitch-black.

Adam Clutterbuck (9)
St Chad's CE Primary School, Winsford

Anger

Anger is like guts in the palm of my hand.
Anger is like an evil brass band playing a deadly tune.
Anger is like the deadly smell of burning.
Anger is like an evil robot turning.
Anger is like a really powerful gunshot going off.
Anger is like a really terrible cough.
Anger is like seeing someone dying.
Anger is like seeing a body frying.

Kieran Sullivan (9)
St Chad's CE Primary School, Winsford

Happy

Happy is like a soft touch of beautiful snow falling from the sky.
Happy is like a good, amazing smell of girl's body spray.
Happy is like animals and children playing on the snowy ground.
Happy is like a nice, tasty meal after a hard day's work.
Happy is like a nice sound that I can hear from a distance.

Sophie O'Grady (9)
St Chad's CE Primary School, Winsford

The Dragon's Treasure

His body was a tortoise shell holding the treasure,
His long, pointed fingers like an eagle's talons grasping the treasure,
His head was an ogre watching the treasure,
The dragon is a guardian of the treasure.

Darren Smith (9)
St Chad's CE Primary School, Winsford

Anger

Anger is running blood through your veins.
Anger is a hot chilli in your mouth.
Anger is a dead body on the floor.
Anger is smoke up your nose.
Anger is blood in your hand.
Anger is a gun in your hand.
Anger is a ball of flaming fire.

Dean Hassall (9)
St Chad's CE Primary School, Winsford

Anger

Anger is a cut too sore to touch.
Anger is the smell of cow muck.
Anger is seeing poor, defenceless animals getting killed.
Anger is the taste of red-hot chillles.
Anger is an alarm going off in my head.

Abigail Evans (9)
St Chad's CE Primary School, Winsford

Crazy

Crazy is like the sun so bright.
Crazy is some sweet sugar.
Crazy is like sherbet running through my mouth.
Crazy is hearing the TV break down.
Crazy is my brain exploding.
Crazy is a popadom popping in my mouth.

Jordan Johnson (9)
St Chad's CE Primary School, Winsford

Calm

Being calm is feeling a giant silky rabbit
brushing through your legs,
Being calm is smelling freshly cut grass
on a Sunday afternoon.
Being calm is like watching clouds go by
on a summer's day.
Being calm is like hearing dolphins squeaking,
talking to each other.
Being calm is tasting fruit salad that your gran makes.

Calm is like no other feeling!

Emma Robinson (9)
St Chad's CE Primary School, Winsford

Anger

Anger is like touching a painful cut on my knee.
Anger is like seeing the fire rise in my head.
Anger is like smelling smoke.
Anger is like tasting red-hot chillies in my mouth, burning.
Anger is like hearing nails down a blackboard.

Rachel Munnerly (9)
St Chad's CE Primary School, Winsford

Anger

Anger is like hot water on my hand,
Anger is voices in my head.
Anger is blood on my hand.
Anger is people screaming.
Anger is eating old food.

Ethan Goodier (9)
St Chad's CE Primary School, Winsford

Anger

I feel anger as a flaming hot fire that starts like a light,
I taste anger as a burgundy, fiery chilli.
I feel anger as a bomb whose rope on the end
is cracking as it burns.
I hear anger as blood goes drip-drop, drip-drop
off that child over there.
I feel anger as a gun's bullet goes right through me.
I feel anger is a very harsh thing.

Emily Kate Baddeley (9)
St Chad's CE Primary School, Winsford

Anger

Anger is like a terrifying fire burning in my hands,
Anger is the smell of a burning outrageous fire.
Anger is a terrible hot chilli, burning in my mouth.
Anger is like a bellowing alarm bell down my ears.
Anger is like seeing a horrid fire rushing down the street.

Rebecca Duckett (9)
St Chad's CE Primary School, Winsford

Nasty

Nasty is the bad smell of gas,
Nasty is the horrible taste of blood.
Nasty is a prickly touch of a sharp knife.
Nasty is seeing a horrible ghost.
Nasty is hearing a big gunshot.

Lauren Cheetham (9)
St Chad's CE Primary School, Winsford

Anger

Anger is like blood dripping down the wall,
Anger is like roaring fires, not stopping at all.
Anger is a dead body in the attic,
Someone getting killed with powerful static.
Anger is screaming in your head,
You walk into a room and see someone dead.
Anger is blood all around everywhere,
See a dead man in his underwear.
Anger is like a gun in your hand,
Seeing someone dead, lying in the sand.

Connor Adamson (9)
St Chad's CE Primary School, Winsford

Joyful

Joyful is the sweet runny taste of ice cream,
Joyful is the sound of cute little bluebirds singing.
Joyful is the smell of yummy, runny chocolate.
Joyful is the feeling of nice, fluffy feathers, all soft and pretty.
Joyful is the sight of happy children, playing in the playground.

Hannah Stacey Done (9)
St Chad's CE Primary School, Winsford

Anger

Anger is touching a cold gun,
Anger is smelling cloudy smoke around you,
Anger is tasting red-hot chilli sauce.
Anger is hearing a waiting bomb go off in a giant city.
Anger is seeing someone stealing from a shop.

Grace Robinson (9)
St Chad's CE Primary School, Winsford

From A Railway Carriage

Out of the station with a boom and a rattle,
With loads of people having a battle.

Faster than wolves, faster than bears
We see people go down the stairs.

Baby in a pram with her gorgeous mother,
The mother's son is the baby's brother.

There goes some bushes, branches and trees,
On the other side, a boy bumps his knees.

There are some people, girls and boys,
They are playing with their toys.

People sitting down on benches,
Looking over bright red fences.

There's a child who loves playing with daisies,
There is the corn to make the mazes.

There is the sun and here comes the rain,
What a pity, it's such a pain.

Ferrari goes past, *zoom za zoom,*
Old banger goes past, *boom ba boom.*

There's a car that's been knocked off the road,
Here's a lorry with a big, heavy load.

There are some buses and here are some trees,
There are some birds and here are some bees.

All of the sights of the wide open plain,
Now it's beginning to rain.

All through the day the light is so bright,
All through the night the vampires bite.

Train through the fields and train on the track,
Into the cave, a hole of pitch-black.

Into the station, back to your home,
Thinking of sights and an ice cream cone.

Year 5 (9)
St Chad's CE Primary School, Winsford

Up In The Attic

Boxed up baby clothes
Packed up play toys
Remains of a pram
My old baby toys.

Old books scattered everywhere
Dad's very old CDs
Very old teddies all sat down
All of my old money boxes
My Thomas beanbag
My very old rusty bed
And my best teddy.

Samuel Harris (8)
St Mary's CE Primary School, Radstock

Up In The Attic

I've got a dusty old Christmas tree,
A big spider's web,
A dusty doll,
And some old toilet rolls,
Some old cobwebby toys,
Some were girls and some were boys.

Chloe Snee (8)
St Mary's CE Primary School, Radstock

Up In The Attic!

Piled boxes
Full of dust
With little woolly suits.
Little black bags filled with
Teddies and knitted shoes.
Lots of wood piled in one big clump
With one raggy doll covered in
Cobwebs and mouldy spiders too.
Five raggy chairs with mould and missing legs.
Fluffy wool under the rotted wood
And lots of wood missing too.

Holly Henderson (9)
St Mary's CE Primary School, Radstock

Up In The Attic

A dusty old PS1 and a big bag
Of PS1 games with two
Nintendoes and small
Socks and dirty old
Clocks and scary spiders
And dusty toy fighters
And an old bike and my sister's
Old trike.

Mitchell Williams (8)
St Mary's CE Primary School, Radstock

Under My Stairs

There is a box covered in dust in the dark with my
Christmas tree in, we put up for Christmas,
There is old book bags covered in dust
In the far corner in the dark,
We hang our coats in the cupboard
Under the stairs on a hook,
We keep our dusty old shoes that don't
Fit anymore in the bit of the cupboard,
We keep our clean shiny shoes at the
Front that we wear nearly every day.

Georgia Nash (9)
St Mary's CE Primary School, Radstock

Up In The Attic

Up in the attic
Boxes in stacks, some squashed flat.
Old fairy lights, half of them missing,
A whole heap of books in the corner, with pages missing.
Old lumps of damp wood,
A dusty lampshade full of holes, it swung back and forth in the wind.
A large jack-in-the-box, so dusty, it's chalky white,
You might see a family of bats.

Nicola Varney (9)
St Mary's CE Primary School, Radstock

The Mysterious Attic

I have spiders
They're such great hiders
Especially in the attic

Betty the bat wears a great big hat
She hangs on the beams and sits on the mats

Monty the moth lives in the loft,
He likes to eat cloth but it gives him a cough

Bertie the blackbird who lives in the gutter
Who flies around all day, trying to collect his supper.

Amie Davis (9)
St Mary's CE Primary School, Radstock

Up In The Attic

My attic
In the dark,
In the dusty attic,
Boxed Christmas tree,
Bags of soft toys,
More sparkling Christmas lights,
Old baby boy dolls,
Boxed up 1980's CDs,
Big, fat, black, juicy spiders,
Up in the creepy attic!

Laila Morris (9)
St Mary's CE Primary School, Radstock

Up In The Attic

In the dark
In the dust
Boxed old toys
And lots of old clothes
Lots of old boxes
Old tangled fairy lights
Cobwebby books
Dusty old creaky floorboards
Smashed dusty bottles
Old sewing machine.

Jessica Butler (9)
St Mary's CE Primary School, Radstock

Up In The Attic

There are bats sleeping
And a dusty old bike
Little mice creeping,
An old creepy floor
Old boxed up china
And a rubbish broken door
Ancient cobwebby treasure
Big bags of leather
Dead rats in the corners
And ripped kids' clothes.

Seth Durham (8)
St Mary's CE Primary School, Radstock

The Writer Of This Poem

(Based on 'The Writer Of This Poem' by Roger McGough)

The writer of this poem is as wiggly as a worm,
The writer of this poem is as feathery as a fern!
The writer of this poem is as stupid as a fly,
The writer of this poem is an MI6 spy!

The writer of this poem is as hairy as a bear,
The writer of this poem is as pointless as a dare!
The writer of this poem is as prickly as a nettle,
The writer of this poem is as hot as a kettle!

The writer of this poem is as giant as a palace,
The writer of this poem is as noisy as me and Alice!
The writer of this poem is as bald as an egg,
The writer of this poem is as skinny as a peg!

The writer of this poem is as buzzy as a bee,
The writer of this poem is as jumpy as a flea!
The writer of this poem is as jokey as a prank,
The writer of this poem is sudden as a . . . yank!

Hannah Lodge (9)
St Wilfred's RCVA Primary School, Bishop Auckland

I Hate School

I hate school
It is cruel.
Maths I hate
But PE is great,
Literacy is bad
It makes me mad.

Jacob Grimshaw (9)
Twiss Green Community Primary School, Warrington

A Recipe For Disaster

Put the:
Lizard legs
Snakes' eggs
And frog stew
Into the brew.

Boil it for three weeks
Leave it till the cauldron leaks
When it does boil it over
Then add rats all the way from Dover.

Go to choir and sing out of tune
Walk under a ladder then spell doom,
Take the potion once a day
For the rest of your life, nothing will go your way.

Elen Shaw (9)
Twiss Green Community Primary School, Warrington

Happiness

The ripple of the wind through the leaves on the trees,
The rustling of bushes when autumn time comes,
The scratching of pencils when we're doing maths sums.
If it wasn't for ears, then no one could hear all these noises.
The Andes mountains in Peru,
A farmer's wife mouthing 'Shoo.'
The waggling of an animal's tail in the zoo,
If it wasn't for eyes, then we would have no sight
To see all the sights that we see.

Rebecca Reed (10)
Twiss Green Community Primary School, Warrington

April Fool's Day

It's the first day of April,
And it tastes of spring,
Like it smells of flowers,
Breathing in the meadow,
Like a golden ring.

Nicola Bailey (9)
Twiss Green Community Primary School, Warrington

The Bully

I can smell the bully,
I fear him,
He feels like a bumpy tree,
He tastes like one too!
He is always angry,
He *loves* all the girls,
He is never sad,
Because he *always* beats up children,
That makes him laugh!
I can smell the bully,
He smells like rotten eggs!

James Martin (9)
Twiss Green Community Primary School, Warrington

Smell

I had anger in my face
I could smell it up my
Nose, it just wouldn't
Go away.

Andrew Gormley (9)
Twiss Green Community Primary School, Warrington

Our Senses

I have ears to listen with and
I see with my eyes and
I smell the scent of the apple pie
Now I feel the breeze against my face.

Alex Chohan (10)
Twiss Green Community Primary School, Warrington

Fear!

We all have a fear,
Whether it's spiders, your exams or heights,
Some are afraid of monsters,
Or ghosts at night!

Some are afraid of others,
And some don't like the dark,
Especially when the moon comes out,
And dogs begin to bark!

Some people just don't like touching,
People don't like what they've got,
Some fear going down a slide,
But others fear the lot!

Jenna Hindmarch (9)
Twiss Green Community Primary School, Warrington

Anger

Anger is like a burning hot flame
Anger is the world's eruption
Anger is shouting, screaming over the air
Anger is people who always swear.

Henry Buttress (9)
Twiss Green Community Primary School, Warrington

Anger

Anger is red
It can sometimes
Make you feel sad.
You can't buy anger
But you can see it
On someone's face.

Bronte Johnston (9)
Twiss Green Community Primary School, Warrington

Fear

I'm terrified of the dark
I can hear myself shivering
All night long
Until dawn breaks.

Matthew Stott (9)
Twiss Green Community Primary School, Warrington

Anger

Anger is a fiery red ball
Which burns around inside you
It takes over your body
When you are mad.

Jack Sheridan (9)
Twiss Green Community Primary School, Warrington

Teachers

I can hear the teacher telling off Jack,
I can smell my school dinner,
I can see my mum,
Coming to pick me up from school.

Rory Quinn (9)
Twiss Green Community Primary School, Warrington

Horrible School!

I hate the iron school gate
As the shadow looms near,
I've never liked the sound of school
It's worse now I'm here.

I don't like the teachers
All they do is shout,
All I'd like to do is play
Instead of work all night, all day.

William Kaye (9)
Twiss Green Community Primary School, Warrington

The Whispering Wind

The wind flies past,
Like when a soul floats to Heaven.
The anger I carry
Is like a volcano erupting,
The hatred I share with my enemy,
And he is the one who brings anger to me.

Jack Keery (9)
Twiss Green Community Primary School, Warrington

Frozen Night

Walking through the frozen night,
It seems to her she had no fright,
Through the air people stare,
But still she doesn't care.

Going in a little house,
Soon she sees a small mouse,
But still she has no fright,
Just to turn on the light.

Hannah Forshaw (9)
Twiss Green Community Primary School, Warrington

Happy I Can

I can feel a flower
I can see a train
I can hear my mum shouting at me
I can smell the person next to me
I can taste my pizza in my mouth
All these things are really good
I can do them but can you?

Sam Watmore (9)
Twiss Green Community Primary School, Warrington

Anger

Anger is the Devil's work,
Bubbling up inside,
Anger gets people hurt,
Which always bugs your
Mind!

Jenny Muirhead (9)
Twiss Green Community Primary School, Warrington

Touch

I touch my heart inside
It is bumping fast
I feel touchiness on my back
I look behind there is nothing there,
I stand and stare.

Katie Brookes (9)
Twiss Green Community Primary School, Warrington

My Love

Your soul is as white as the feather on a swan's neck.
Your eyes are as orange as the gazing sunset falls.
She's as fierce as a lioness on the prowl for fresh meat.
Your heart is a soul crying for forgiveness and trust.
She's more braver than bravery itself.
Your more gentler than a drop of rain hitting the river of beauty.
She's got more strength than a bolt of lightning striking.
She's as fun as a puppy dog.

Steven Cornell (10)
Unsworth Primary School, Bury

Autumn Leaves

Orange, red and brown leaves fall from the trees,
The ground is covered by a carpet of leaves,
Autumn leaves fall to the ground,
Whirling, swirling round and round,
The leaves fall to the ground like a sheet,
That crunches and crackles under your feet.

Rebecca Lloyd (10)
Unsworth Primary School, Bury

Alien

A liens arrive in the dark of night,
L urking around scaring everything in sight,
I n a spaceship, they come, with eyes on a stalk,
E veryone of them green and away they walk,
N o one's safe in an alien invasion!

Naomi Park (10)
Unsworth Primary School, Bury

Spotted Leopard

Spotted leopards are about 4 foot tall,
They could jump over a wall,
They can take down a tunnel,
And run through a hall.

Leopards have black spots and orange skin,
They are vicious,
They rummage in other animal's land
They are malicious.

They are predators in grass,
They go up a hill,
Running up it still,
They go for the kill.

Jordan Wheeldon (10)
Unsworth Primary School, Bury

The Tiny Ant

The tiny ant,
Working so hard for its queen,
Small, teeny, microscopic,
Like a piece of dust in a vacuum cleaner,
As small as a germ,
They make me feel huge,
Like the sun towering over the Earth,
The tiny ant,
Every single one has an important job.

Toby Campion (10)
Unsworth Primary School, Bury

Dogs

Dogs are very fluffy,
They have a very loud bark,
Dogs have soft padded feet,
And they go out in the dark.

Dogs adore their brill food,
They dig a hole for a bone,
They run about outside,
And they moan when they're alone.

Dogs are cuddly and soft,
And they chase cats away,
They climb up into the loft,
And like to play all day.

Chloe Bodkin (10)
Unsworth Primary School, Bury

Lovely Holidays

A holiday
It's enjoyable
Joyful, amazing, lazy,
Like a break in your life,
Like a laze in the garden,
It makes me feel very happy,
Like a giddy puppy,
A holiday,
How lucky we are.

Rebecca Cooper (10)
Unsworth Primary School, Bury

Rolly

I have a rabbit called Rolly
He loves playing with me
He runs around the garden
And sits on my knee.

He loves eating carrots
And his rabbit food
He eats it in a second
He really is a rabbit dude.

Rolly's very soft and smooth
I love him very much
His colour is a dark brown
He lives in his rabbit hutch.

Lucy Hill (10)
Unsworth Primary School, Bury